TAPAS

This is a Parragon Book
This edition published in 2005

Parragon
Queen Street House
4 Queen Street
Bath BA1 1HE, UK

Photography: Ian Parsons and David Jordan
Home economists: Jacqueline Bellefontaine, Richard Green,
Kate Mosely and Brian Wilson

ISBN: 1-40544-861-X

Printed in China

Produced by the Bridgewater Book Company Ltd.

NOTE

This book uses metric and imperial measurements. Follow the same
units of measurement throughout; do not mix metric and imperial.
All spoon measurements are level: teaspoons are assumed to be 5 ml,
and tablespoons are assumed to be 15 ml. Unless otherwise stated,
milk is assumed to be full fat, eggs and individual vegetables such
as potatoes are medium, and pepper is freshly ground black pepper.

The times given for each recipe are an approximate guide only
because the cooking times may vary as a result of the types of oven
and other equipment used.

Recipes using raw or very lightly cooked eggs should be
avoided by infants, the elderly, pregnant women, convalescents and
anyone suffering from an illness. Pregnant and breast-feeding women
are advised to avoid eating peanuts and peanut products.

Contents

Introduction

One of the many delights of visiting Spain is the rich tradition of tapas. The origin of tapas is unclear, but one legend has it that tapas was first cooked for King Alfonso X *el Sabio* ('the Wise'), ruler of Castile in the thirteenth century. The king, suffering from an illness, was required to eat  small quantities of food and wine between meals. On his recovery, he advocated that wine was not to be served in inns without something more solid to accompany it.

However, most consider that Andalusia, not Castile, can lay claim to being the birthplace of tapas. In this famous wine-making region, it became customary to serve wine with either a slice of bread covered with ham or cheese, or a saucer with some other food, covering the glass. This acted as a barrier, preventing flies or other impurities contaminating the wine, and so it began to be known after the word 'tapa', which means a cover or lid. From this starting point, tapas spread throughout Spain, and now beyond.

In contemporary Spain, tapas remains an essential and integral part of Spanish lifestyle, usually served between lunch and dinner in cafés and bars with an apéritif, such as wine, sherry or cider. This provides an ideal stopping point for people returning home in the evening, as well as offering the chance for friends and colleagues to unwind at the end of the day. Alternatively, choosing a larger number of dishes can turn the event into an entire meal. The broad variety of tapas reflects these differing needs, with cosas de picar ('little things to nibble') being the simplest finger food – such as a bowl of olives or salted nuts – and pinchos, slightly larger fare, speared on a cocktail stick. At the other end of the scale are raciones, which are larger dishes that can form the basis of a more filling meal.

The range of tapas dishes is vast and is a reflection of the variety of culinary traditions of the different Spanish regions. This book presents a selection of some of the most famous dishes, such as the classic Spanish Tortilla (see page 100) and Tomato Bread (see page 240), as well as lots of regional specialities such as 'Wrinkled' Potatoes with Mojo Sauce (see page 24) from the Canary Islands and Traditional Catalan Salt Cod Salad (see page 124), served in bars in Barcelona.

Tapas is no longer the preserve of Spain, with numerous tapas bars and restaurants springing up in cosmopolitan cities throughout the world. It is also becoming increasingly popular to make and enjoy at home.

Part of the appeal of tapas is that eating them can be one of the most social ways of dining with friends and family, particularly when eaten as a main meal, with everyone sampling the wide range of dishes at the table. The fact that so many hot and cold dishes can be eaten alongside each other also makes it one of the more eclectic eating experiences. It is not often that you can take a couple of bites of a fish dish before sampling a chorizo empanadilla, all accompanied by a glass of wine and a few marinated olives. You can let your taste buds guide you to whatever sort of dish you fancy next!

Key Ingredients

Cheese

There are numerous cheeses produced in Spain, though the vast majority are limited in availability to the region where they are produced. Manchego, made from sheep's milk, is probably the most well-known Spanish cheese and is widely available. Many other Spanish cheeses are used in the recipes in this book, but acceptable, more common substitutes are also suggested.

Chorizo sausage

Chorizo is one of the best known and most widely available Spanish sausages. It is made from pork (smoked or unsmoked) and seasoned with paprika. It can be bought in various different sizes and with varying quantities of fat.

Garlic

Garlic is a key ingredient in Spanish cooking. Garlic bulbs should be stored in a cool, dry place, and once a head of garlic has been broken into, the cloves should be used within 10 days, before they dry out. When buying garlic, look for firm heads with a tight, white outer skin.

Ham

Ham is a staple of Spanish cuisine, and hams have been produced for at least 2,000 years. The quality of ham is dependent on the maturation period, and the best hams, and most expensive, are often hand-sliced. They are suitable for being served raw as tapas. Less expensive ham can be used when cooked. Italian prosciutto can be used instead. Serrano ham is a generic term for cuts of leg meat from pigs from the mountain regions. These hams are salt-cured and breeze-dried.

Olive oil

Spain is the largest producer of olive oil in the world, so it is no surprise that it is also the cornerstone of Spanish cuisine. The best quality olive oil is extra virgin, which is the first cold pressing and should be saved for dressings and marinades rather than used for frying. Virgin is less refined than extra virgin. A blend of virgin and refined oils is known simply as 'olive oil', though it is not as widely exported as the other varieties.

Olives

It is perhaps no coincidence that olives, a staple of tapas and eaten alone or used in more complex dishes, are a key produce of Andalusia. Over half of the 50 varieties of olive grown in Spain for eating come from this region. Some of the dishes in this book use olives stuffed with pimientos – a large, heart-shaped pepper.

Paprika

Spanish paprika, the finely ground powder of dried red pepper, is normally milder than the central European paprika, though occasionally much hotter varieties are used.

Basic Recipes

fried potatoes

SERVES 6

1 kg/2 lb 4 oz potatoes, unpeeled

olive oil

sea salt

1 Scrub the potatoes, pat them dry and cut into chunky pieces.

2 Put 1 cm/½ inch olive oil and 1 potato piece in 1 or 2 large, heavy-based frying pans over a medium–high heat and heat until the potato begins to sizzle. Add the remaining potatoes, without crowding the pans, and fry for 15 minutes, or until golden brown all over and tender. Work in batches, if necessary, keeping the cooked potatoes warm while you fry the remainder.

3 Use a slotted spoon to transfer the potatoes to a plate covered with crumpled kitchen paper. Blot off any excess oil and sprinkle with sea salt. Serve immediately.

tomato & pepper salsa

MAKES 700 ML/1¼ PINTS

4 tbsp olive oil

10 large garlic cloves

140 g/5 oz shallots, chopped

4 large red peppers, deseeded
    and chopped

1 kg/2 lb 4 oz ripe, fresh
    tomatoes, chopped, or
    1.2 kg/2 lb 12 oz good-quality
    canned chopped tomatoes

2 thin strips freshly pared
    orange rind

pinch of hot red pepper flakes,
    to taste (optional)

salt and pepper

1 Heat the olive oil in a large, flameproof casserole over a medium heat. Add the garlic, shallots and peppers and fry for 10 minutes, stirring occasionally, until the peppers are softened, but not browned.

2 Add the tomatoes, including the juices if using canned ones, orange rind, hot pepper flakes, if using, and salt and pepper to taste and bring to the boil. Reduce the heat to as low as possible and simmer, uncovered, for 45 minutes, or until the liquid evaporates and the sauce thickens.

3 Purée the sauce through a mouli. Alternatively, purée in a food processor, then use a wooden spoon to press through a fine sieve. Taste and adjust the seasoning if necessary. Use immediately, or cover and leave to chill for up to 3 days.

Vegetables

The recipes in this chapter are a mixture of vegetable and vegetarian dishes that are a delicious bite-to-eat in their own right, and others that would make great side dishes to some of the recipes contained elsewhere in this book. There is a wide variety of potato dishes – always a staple of tapas menus – including the ever-popular Baby Potatoes with Aïoli (see page 12) and the Catalan classic, Feisty Potatoes (see page 15). As its name suggests, the latter uses a hot sauce to spice up fried potatoes with aïoli.

Other tapas dishes include the delightful, bite-sized Stuffed Cherry Tomatoes (see page 38), the slightly more substantial Courgettes with Cheese & Vinaigrette (see page 43), and a range of tasty salads.

spanish potatoes

serves four

2 tbsp olive oil

500 g/1 lb 2 oz small new
   potatoes, halved

1 onion, halved and sliced

1 green pepper, deseeded and
   cut into strips

1 tsp chilli powder

1 tsp mustard

300 ml/10 fl oz passata

300 ml/10 fl oz vegetable stock

salt and pepper

chopped fresh parsley, to garnish

1 Heat the olive oil in a large, heavy-based frying pan. Add the new potatoes and sliced onion and cook, stirring frequently, for 4–5 minutes, or until the onion slices are soft and translucent.

2 Add the pepper strips, chilli powder and mustard to the frying pan and cook for 2–3 minutes.

3 Stir the passata and vegetable stock into the frying pan and bring to the boil. Reduce the heat and leave to simmer for 25 minutes, or until the potatoes are tender. Season to taste with salt and pepper.

4 Transfer the potatoes to a warmed serving dish. Sprinkle the chopped parsley over the top and serve immediately.

5 Alternatively, leave the potatoes to cool completely and serve cold, at room temperature.

new potatoes with chilli sauce

serves four–six

450 g/1 lb new potatoes, unpeeled

2 garlic cloves, chopped

2 dried red chillies, lightly crushed

1 tbsp paprika

2 tbsp sherry vinegar

150 ml/5 fl oz olive oil

salt

1 Place the potatoes in a steamer set over a saucepan of boiling water. Cover and steam for 30 minutes, or until tender.

2 Meanwhile, make the sauce. Place the garlic, chillies and paprika in a mortar and grind to a paste with a pestle. Season to taste with salt, then gradually work in the vinegar. Finally, work in the olive oil.

3 Transfer the potatoes to warmed serving dishes and serve immediately, handing round the chilli sauce separately.

VARIATION

You can substitute 1 deseeded and finely chopped fresh red chilli for the dried chillies if you prefer. Stir it into the sauce at the end of Step 2.

baby potatoes with aïoli

serves six–eight

450 g/1 lb baby new potatoes

1 tbsp chopped fresh
   flat-leaf parsley

salt

AÏOLI

1 large egg yolk, at room
   temperature

1 tbsp white wine vinegar or
   lemon juice

2 large garlic cloves, peeled

5 tbsp Spanish extra virgin
   olive oil

5 tbsp sunflower oil

salt and pepper

1 To make the Aïoli, place the egg yolk, vinegar or lemon juice, garlic and salt and pepper to taste in a food processor fitted with a metal blade and blend together. With the motor still running, very slowly add the olive oil, then the sunflower oil, drop by drop at first, then, when it begins to thicken, in a slow, steady stream until the sauce is thick and smooth. Alternatively, use a bowl and whisk to make the Aïoli.

2 For this recipe, the Aïoli should be quite thin to coat the potatoes. To ensure this, blend in 1 tablespoon water to form the consistency of sauce.

3 To prepare the potatoes, cut them in half or quarters to make bite-sized pieces. If they are very small, you can leave them whole. Place the potatoes in a large saucepan of cold salted water and bring to the boil. Reduce the heat and simmer for 7 minutes, or until just tender. Drain well, then transfer to a large bowl.

4 While the potatoes are still warm, pour over the Aïoli sauce and gently toss the potatoes in it. Adding the sauce to the potatoes while they are still warm will help them to absorb the garlic flavour. Leave for 20 minutes to allow the potatoes to marinate in the sauce.

5 Transfer the potatoes with Aïoli to a warmed serving dish, sprinkle over the parsley and salt to taste and serve warm. Alternatively, the dish can be prepared ahead and stored in the refrigerator, but return it to room temperature before serving.

ham-wrapped potatoes

serves four

12 new potatoes, unpeeled

2 tbsp olive oil

12 slices serrano ham

salt

1 Preheat the oven to 200°C/
400°F/Gas Mark 6. Place the
potatoes in a steamer set over a
saucepan of boiling water. Cover and
steam for 30 minutes, or until tender.
Remove from the heat and leave to
cool slightly.

2 Pour the olive oil into an
ovenproof dish. Wrap each
potato in a slice of ham and arrange
in the dish in a single layer. Roast in
the preheated oven, turning
occasionally, for 20 minutes.

3 Transfer the potatoes to warmed
serving dishes, season to taste
with salt and serve immediately or
leave to cool a little before serving.

COOK'S TIP
Try to find potatoes that are all
about the same size so that they
cook evenly.

feisty potatoes

serves six

1 x quantity Fried Potatoes
  (see page 7)
1 x quantity Aïoli
  (see page 12)
CHILLI OIL
150 ml/5 fl oz olive oil
2 small hot fresh red chillies, slit
1 tsp hot Spanish paprika

1 To make the chilli oil, heat the olive oil and chillies over a high heat until the chillies begin to sizzle. Remove the pan from the heat and stir in the paprika. Set aside and leave to cool, then transfer the chilli oil to a pourer with a spout. Do not strain.

2 Fry the potatoes, and while they cook make the Aïoli.

3 To serve, divide the potatoes between 6 serving plates and add a dollop of Aïoli to each. Drizzle with chilli oil and serve warm or at room temperature. In Spain these are served with wooden cocktail sticks.

COOK'S TIP

You will find as many
'authentic' recipes for this dish
as there are cooks in Spain:
sometimes the potatoes
are deep-fried, and often
the Aïoli and chilli oil are
mixed together.

peppered potatoes

serves six–eight

900 g/2 lb new potatoes, unpeeled

125 ml/4 fl oz olive oil

1 tbsp sherry vinegar

1 tbsp sun-dried tomato purée

1 tsp paprika

pinch of cayenne pepper

salt

1 Place the potatoes in a large saucepan of lightly salted water and bring to the boil. Reduce the heat, cover and leave to simmer for 15–20 minutes, or until just tender. Drain and leave to cool.

2 Meanwhile, make the sauce. Mix 5 tablespoons of the olive oil, the vinegar, tomato purée, paprika and cayenne pepper together in a large bowl and season to taste with salt. Reserve until required.

3 Heat the remaining olive oil in a large, heavy-based frying pan. Cut the potatoes into quarters and add to the pan, in batches if necessary. Cook over a medium heat, stirring and turning occasionally, for 8–10 minutes, or until crisp and golden brown. Drain with a slotted spoon and add to the bowl containing the sauce.

4 When all the potatoes have been cooked, toss gently in the sauce, then divide between warmed serving dishes. Serve immediately.

fried potatoes with piquant paprika

serves six

3 tsp paprika

1 tsp ground cumin

¼–½ tsp cayenne pepper

½ tsp salt

450 g/1 lb small old potatoes,
   peeled

sunflower oil, for shallow-frying

fresh parsley sprigs, to garnish

Aïoli (see page 12), to serve
   (optional)

1 Place the paprika, ground cumin, cayenne pepper and salt into a small bowl. Mix well together and reserve.

VARIATION

Fry the potatoes as here, then spoon over the Fiery Tomato Salsa that accompanies the Cheese Puffs (see page 112), or serve the salsa separately for dipping the potatoes in. This dish is then known as Patatas Bravas (Bold Potatoes).

2 Cut each potato into 8 thick wedges. Pour enough sunflower oil into a large, heavy-based frying pan so that it comes about 2.5 cm/1 inch up the sides of the frying pan. Heat the oil, then add the potato wedges, preferably in a single layer, and fry gently for 10 minutes, or until golden brown all over, turning occasionally. Remove from the frying pan with a slotted spoon and drain on kitchen paper.

3 Transfer the potato wedges to a large bowl and, while they are still hot, sprinkle with the paprika mixture, then gently toss them together to coat.

4 Turn the fried potatoes with paprika into one large, warmed serving dish, several smaller ones or individual serving plates and serve hot, garnished with parsley sprigs. Accompany with a bowl of Aïoli for dipping, if wished.

warm potato salad

serves four–six

175 ml/6 fl oz olive oil

450 g/1 lb waxy potatoes,
    thinly sliced

50 ml/2 fl oz white wine vinegar

2 garlic cloves, finely chopped

salt and pepper

COOK'S TIP

If serving this salad with a platter
of mixed tapas, either combine
with other warm dishes or leave
it to cool before serving.

1 Heat 50 ml/2 fl oz of the olive oil in a large, heavy-based frying pan. Add the potato slices, season to taste with salt and cook over a low heat, shaking the pan occasionally, for 10 minutes. Turn the potatoes over and cook for a further 5 minutes, or until tender but not browned.

2 Meanwhile, pour the vinegar into a small saucepan. Add the garlic and season to taste with pepper. Bring to the boil, then stir in the remaining olive oil.

3 Transfer the potatoes to a bowl and pour over the dressing. Toss gently and leave to stand for 15 minutes. Using a slotted spoon, transfer the potatoes to individual serving dishes and serve warm.

russian salad

serves six

2 eggs

450 g/1 lb baby new potatoes,
    quartered

115 g/4 oz fine green beans, cut
    into 2.5-cm/1-inch lengths

115 g/4 oz frozen peas

115 g/4 oz carrots

200 g/7 oz canned tuna in olive
    oil, drained

8 tbsp mayonnaise

2 tbsp lemon juice

1 garlic clove, crushed

4 small gherkins, sliced

8 stoned black olives, halved

1 tbsp capers

1 tbsp chopped fresh
    flat-leaf parsley

1 tbsp chopped fresh dill, plus extra
    sprigs to garnish

salt and pepper

1 Place the eggs in a saucepan, cover with cold water and slowly bring to the boil. Immediately reduce the heat to very low, cover and simmer gently for 10 minutes. As soon as the eggs are cooked, drain them and place under cold running water until they are cold. By doing this quickly, you will prevent a black ring forming around the egg yolk. Gently tap the eggs to crack the eggshells and leave to stand until cold.

2 Meanwhile, place the potatoes in a large saucepan of cold, salted water and bring to the boil. Reduce the heat and simmer for 7 minutes, or until just tender. Add the beans and peas to the saucepan for the last 2 minutes of cooking. Drain well, splash under cold running water, then leave the vegetables to cool completely.

3 Cut the carrots into julienne strips about 2.5 cm/1 inch in length. Flake the tuna into large chunks. When the potatoes, beans and peas are cold, place them in a large bowl. Add the carrot strips and the flaked tuna and very gently toss the ingredients together. Transfer the vegetables and tuna to a large salad bowl or serving dish.

4 Place the mayonnaise in a jug, then stir in the lemon juice to thin it slightly. Stir in the garlic and season to taste with salt and pepper. Drizzle the mayonnaise dressing over the vegetables and tuna.

5 Sprinkle the gherkins, olives and capers into the salad and finally sprinkle over the parsley and dill. You can store the salad in the refrigerator but return to room temperature before serving. Just before serving, shell the eggs and slice into wedges. Add the eggs to the salad, then garnish with dill sprigs and serve.

potato wedges with roasted garlic dip

serves eight

1.3 kg/3 lb potatoes, unpeeled
and halved

2 tbsp olive oil

1 garlic clove, finely chopped

2 tsp salt

ROASTED GARLIC DIP

2 garlic bulbs, separated into cloves

1 tbsp olive oil

5 tbsp crème fraîche or Greek-style
yogurt

4 tbsp mayonnaise

paprika, to taste

salt

VARIATION

You can also serve the potato
wedges with Aïoli (see page 12)
or simply with good-quality
mayonnaise, if you are in a hurry.

1 First, make the roasted garlic
dip. Preheat the oven to 200°C/
400°F/Gas Mark 6. Place the garlic
cloves in an ovenproof dish, pour in
the olive oil and toss to coat. Spread
out in a single layer and roast in the
preheated oven for 25 minutes,
or until tender. Remove from the oven
and leave until cool enough to handle.

2 Peel the garlic cloves, then place
on a heavy chopping board and
sprinkle with a little salt. Mash well
with a fork until smooth. Scrape into
a bowl and stir in the crème fraîche
or yogurt and mayonnaise. Season to
taste with salt and paprika. Cover the
bowl with clingfilm and leave to chill
until ready to serve.

3 To cook the potatoes, cut each
potato half into 3 wedges and
place in a large bowl. Add the olive
oil, garlic and salt and toss well.
Transfer the wedges to a roasting tin,
arrange in a single layer and roast in
the preheated oven for 1–1¼ hours,
or until crisp and golden.

4 Remove from the oven and
transfer to serving bowls.
Serve immediately, handing round
the roasted garlic dip separately.

'wrinkled' potatoes with mojo sauce

serves four–six

70 g/2½ oz sea salt

24 small, new red-skinned
   potatoes, unpeeled and
   kept whole

MOJO SAUCE

40 g/1½ oz day-old bread,
   crusts removed and torn into
   small pieces

2 large garlic cloves

½ tsp salt

1½ tbsp hot Spanish paprika

1 tbsp ground cumin

about 2 tbsp red wine vinegar

about 5 tbsp extra virgin olive oil

2 pimientos del piquillo (see page
   160), drained

1 Pour about 2.5 cm/1 inch of water into a saucepan and stir in the sea salt. Add the potatoes and stir again. They do not have to be covered with water. Fold a clean tea towel to fit over the potatoes, then bring the water to the boil. Reduce the heat and leave to simmer for 20 minutes, or until the potatoes are tender, but still holding together.

2 Remove the tea towel and reserve. Drain the potatoes and return them to the empty saucepan. When the tea towel is cool enough to handle, wring the saltwater it contains into the saucepan. Place the saucepan over a low heat and shake until the potatoes are dry and coated with a thin white film. Remove from the heat.

3 Meanwhile, make the Mojo Sauce. Place the bread in a bowl, add just enough water to cover and leave to stand for 5 minutes to soften. Use your hands to squeeze all the water from the bread. Use a pestle and mortar to mash the garlic and salt into a paste. Stir in the paprika and

cumin. Transfer to a food processor. Add 2 tablespoons of vinegar and blend, then add the bread and 2 tablespoons of olive oil and blend again.

4 With the motor still running, add the peppers one at a time. Blend until they are puréed and a sauce forms. Add more olive oil, if necessary, until the sauce is smooth and thick. Taste and adjust the seasoning, adding extra vinegar, if necessary.

5 To serve, cut the potatoes in half and spear with wooden cocktail sticks. Serve with a bowl of sauce on the side for dipping. The potatoes can be eaten hot or at room temperature.

aubergine dip

serves six–eight

1 large aubergine, about
   400 g/14 oz
5 tbsp olive oil
2 spring onions, finely chopped
1 large garlic clove, crushed
2 tbsp finely chopped fresh parsley
salt and pepper
smoked sweet Spanish paprika,
   to garnish
French bread, to serve

1 Cut the aubergine into thick slices and sprinkle with salt to draw out any bitterness. Leave to stand for 30 minutes, then rinse and pat dry.

2 Heat 4 tablespoons of the olive oil in a large frying pan over a medium–high heat. Add the aubergine slices and fry on both sides until soft and beginning to brown. Remove from the frying pan and leave to cool. The slices will release the oil again as they cool.

3 Heat the remaining olive oil in the frying pan. Add the spring onions and garlic and fry for 3 minutes, or until the spring onions become soft. Remove from the heat and reserve with the aubergine slices to cool.

4 Transfer all the ingredients to a food processor and process just until a coarse purée forms. Transfer to a serving bowl and stir in the parsley. Taste and adjust the seasoning, if necessary. Serve immediately, or cover and leave to chill until 15 minutes before required. Sprinkle with paprika and serve with French bread.

25

aubergine & pepper dip

serves six–eight

2 large aubergines

2 red peppers

4 tbsp Spanish olive oil

2 garlic cloves, roughly chopped

grated rind and juice of
½ lemon

1 tbsp chopped fresh coriander,
plus extra sprigs to garnish

½–1 tsp paprika

salt and pepper

bread or toast, to serve

VARIATION

Instead of cooking the aubergines and peppers in the oven, they can be cooked under a preheated grill until the skins are charred all over. They do, however, need to be turned frequently and will take about 10 minutes. This dip is also very good served with cold meats.

1 Preheat the oven to 190°C/ 375°F/Gas Mark 5. Prick the skins of the aubergines and peppers all over with a fork and brush with 1 tablespoon of the olive oil. Place on a baking tray and bake in the preheated oven for 45 minutes, or until the skins are beginning to turn black, the flesh of the aubergine is very soft and the peppers are deflated.

2 When the vegetables are cooked, place them in a bowl and cover tightly with a clean, damp tea towel. Alternatively, place the vegetables in a polythene bag and leave for about 15 minutes until cool enough to handle.

3 When the vegetables have cooled, cut the aubergines in half lengthways, carefully scoop out the flesh and discard the skin. Cut the aubergine flesh into large chunks. Remove and discard the stem, core and seeds from the peppers and cut the flesh into large pieces.

4 Heat the remaining olive oil in a frying pan. Add the aubergine and pepper and fry for 5 minutes. Add the garlic and fry for 30 seconds.

5 Turn the contents of the frying pan onto kitchen paper to drain, then transfer to a food processor. Add the lemon rind and juice, the chopped coriander, the paprika, and salt and pepper to taste, then process until a speckled purée is formed.

6 Transfer the aubergine and pepper dip to a serving bowl. Serve warm, at room temperature, or leave to cool for 30 minutes, then leave to chill in the refrigerator for at least 1 hour, then serve cold. Garnish with coriander sprigs and accompany with thick slices of bread or toast for dipping.

marinated aubergines

2 aubergines, halved lengthways

4 tbsp olive oil

2 garlic cloves, finely chopped

2 tbsp chopped fresh parsley

1 tbsp chopped fresh thyme

2 tbsp lemon juice

salt and pepper

COOK'S TIP

Modern varieties of aubergine rarely contain bitter juices, so there is less need to salt them than in the past.

1 Make 2–3 slashes in the flesh of the aubergine halves and place, cut-side down, in an ovenproof dish. Season to taste with salt and pepper, pour over the olive oil and sprinkle with the garlic, parsley and thyme. Cover and leave to marinate at room temperature for 2–3 hours.

2 Preheat the oven to 180°C/350°F/ Gas Mark 4. Uncover the dish and roast the aubergines in the preheated oven for 45 minutes. Remove the dish from the oven and turn the aubergines over. Baste with the cooking juices and sprinkle with the lemon juice. Return to the oven and cook for a further 15 minutes.

3 Transfer the aubergines to serving plates. Spoon over the cooking juices and serve hot or warm.

sweet onion salad

serves four–six

4 Spanish onions

2 tbsp chopped fresh parsley

115 g/4 oz black olives, stoned

1 tbsp sherry vinegar

2 tbsp red wine vinegar

125 ml/4 fl oz olive oil

about 1 tbsp water

salt and pepper

1 Bring a large saucepan of lightly salted water to the boil. Add the onions and simmer for 20 minutes, or until tender. Drain and leave until cool enough to handle.

2 Thickly slice the onions and place in a shallow dish. Sprinkle over the parsley and olives and season to taste with pepper.

3 Whisk the vinegars and olive oil together in a bowl, then whisk in enough of the water to make a creamy vinaigrette.

4 Pour the dressing over the onions and serve at room temperature.

COOK'S TIP

Spanish onions are both large and mild. If you are unable to find them, substitute red or white onions, which are also sweet. They tend to be smaller, so you may need 5 or 6.

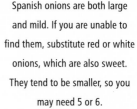

baked stuffed onions

serves four

4 large Spanish onions

2 slices streaky bacon, diced

½ red pepper, halved, deseeded
   and diced

125 g/4½ oz fresh lean beef mince

1 tbsp chopped mixed fresh herbs,
   such as parsley, thyme and
   rosemary or 1 tsp dried
   mixed herbs

25 g/1 oz fresh white breadcrumbs

butter, for greasing

300 ml/10 fl oz beef stock

salt and pepper

cooked long-grain rice, garnished
   with chopped fresh parsley,
   to serve

GRAVY

25 g/1 oz butter

125 g/4½ oz mushrooms,
   finely chopped

300 ml/10 fl oz beef stock

2 tbsp cornflour

2 tbsp water

1 Preheat the oven to 180°C/
350°F/Gas Mark 4. Place the
onions in a saucepan of lightly salted
water, then bring to the boil. Reduce
the heat and leave to simmer for
15 minutes, or until tender.

2 Remove the onions from the
saucepan, drain and cool slightly,
then hollow out the centres and finely
chop the inner flesh.

3 Heat a frying pan and cook
the bacon until the fat runs out.
Add the chopped onion and red
pepper and cook for 5–7 minutes,
stirring frequently.

4 Add the beef to the frying pan
and cook, stirring, for 3 minutes,
until browned. Remove the pan from
the heat and stir in the herbs, and
breadcrumbs. Season to taste with salt
and pepper.

5 Grease an ovenproof dish and
stand the whole onions in it. Pack
the beef mixture into the centres and
pour the stock around them. Bake the
onions in the preheated oven for
1–1½ hours, or until tender.

6 To make the gravy, heat the butter
in a small saucepan. Add the
mushrooms and fry for 3–4 minutes.
Strain the liquid from the onions and
add to the saucepan with the stock,
then cook for 2–3 minutes.

7 Mix the cornflour with the water,
then stir into the gravy and heat,
stirring, until thickened and smooth.
Season to taste with salt and pepper.
Serve the onions with the gravy and
rice, garnished with parsley.

moorish broad bean dip

serves six

500 g/1 lb 2 oz shelled fresh or
   frozen broad beans
5 tbsp olive oil
1 garlic clove, finely chopped
1 onion, finely chopped
1 tsp ground cumin
1 tbsp lemon juice
175 ml/6 fl oz water
1 tbsp chopped fresh mint
salt and pepper
paprika, to garnish
raw vegetables, crusty bread or
   breadsticks, to serve

1 If using fresh broad beans, bring a large saucepan of lightly salted water to the boil. Add the beans, then reduce the heat, cover and simmer for 7 minutes. Drain well, refresh under cold running water and drain again. Remove and discard the outer skins. If using frozen beans, leave to thaw completely, then remove and discard the outer skins.

COOK'S TIP
Classic Arab spices and herbs still feature in modern Spanish cuisine, especially in the south of the country.

2 Heat 1 tablespoon of the olive oil in a frying pan. Add the garlic, onion and cumin and cook over a low heat, stirring occasionally, until the onion is softened and translucent. Add the broad beans and cook, stirring frequently, for 5 minutes.

3 Remove the frying pan from the heat and transfer the mixture to a food processor or blender. Add the lemon juice, the remaining olive oil, water and mint and process to a paste. Season to taste with salt and pepper.

4 Scrape the paste back into the frying pan and heat gently until warm. Transfer to individual serving bowls, dust lightly with paprika and serve with dippers of your choice.

broad beans with cheese & prawns

serves six

500 g/1 lb 2 oz shelled fresh or
   frozen broad beans

2 fresh thyme sprigs

225 g/8 oz cooked peeled prawns

225 g/8 oz Queso Majorero or
   Gruyère cheese, diced

6 tbsp olive oil

2 tbsp lemon juice

1 garlic clove, finely chopped

salt and pepper

1 Bring a large saucepan of lightly salted water to the boil. Add the broad beans and 1 thyme sprig, then reduce the heat, cover and simmer for 7 minutes. Drain well, refresh under cold running water and drain again.

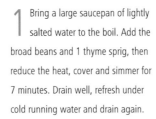

2 Unless the broad beans are very young, remove and discard the outer skins. Place the beans in a bowl and add the prawns and cheese.

3 Chop the remaining thyme sprig. Whisk the olive oil, lemon juice, garlic and chopped thyme together in a separate bowl and season to taste with salt and pepper.

4 Pour the dressing over the bean mixture, toss lightly and serve.

COOK'S TIP

Queso Majorero is a goat's milk cheese from Fuerteventura in the Canary Islands. It has a melt-in-the-mouth texture that goes particularly well with sherry and red wine.

broad beans with serrano ham

serves six–eight

55 g/2 oz serrano or Parma ham,
   pancetta or rindless smoked
   streaky bacon

115 g/4 oz chorizo sausage, outer
   casing removed

4 tbsp Spanish olive oil

1 onion, finely chopped

2 garlic cloves, finely chopped

splash of dry white wine

450 g/1 lb frozen broad beans,
   thawed, or about 1.3 kg/3 lb
   fresh broad beans in their pods,
   shelled to give 450 g/1 lb

1 tbsp chopped fresh dill or mint,
   plus extra to garnish

pinch of sugar

salt and pepper

1 Using a sharp knife, cut the ham into small strips. Cut the chorizo into 2-cm/³⁄₄-inch cubes. Heat the oil in a large, heavy-based frying pan. Add the onion and fry for 5 minutes, or until softened and beginning to brown. If you are using pancetta or bacon, add it with the onion. Add the garlic and fry for a further 30 seconds.

2 Pour the wine into the frying pan, increase the heat and let it bubble to evaporate the alcohol, then reduce the heat. Add the broad beans, ham, if using, and the chorizo and fry for 1–2 minutes, stirring all the time to coat in the oil.

3 Cover the frying pan and let the beans simmer very gently, stirring occasionally, for 10–15 minutes, or until the beans are tender. It may be necessary to add a little water to the pan during cooking, so keep an eye on it and add a splash if the beans appear to become too dry. Stir in the mint or dill and sugar. Season to taste with salt and pepper, but taste first as you may find that it does not need any salt.

4 Transfer the broad beans to a large, warmed serving dish, several smaller ones or individual plates and serve piping hot, garnished with chopped dill.

35

mixed beans

serves four–six

175 g/6 oz shelled fresh or frozen
   broad beans

115 g/4 oz fresh or frozen
   French beans

115 g/4 oz mangetout

1 shallot, finely chopped

6 fresh mint sprigs

4 tbsp olive oil

1 tbsp sherry vinegar

1 garlic clove, finely chopped

salt and pepper

1 Bring a large saucepan of lightly salted water to the boil. Add the broad beans, reduce the heat, cover and simmer for 7 minutes. Remove the beans with a slotted spoon, plunge into cold water and drain. Remove and discard the outer skins.

2 Meanwhile, return the saucepan of salted water to the boil. Add the French beans and return to the boil again. Drain and refresh under cold running water. Drain well.

3 Mix the broad beans, French beans, mangetout and shallot together in a bowl. Strip the leaves from the mint sprigs, reserve half and add the remainder to the bean mixture. Finely chop the reserved mint.

4 Whisk the olive oil, vinegar, garlic and chopped mint together in a separate bowl and season to taste with salt and pepper. Pour the dressing over the bean mixture and toss lightly to coat. Cover with clingfilm and leave to chill until required.

stuffed cherry tomatoes

serves eight

24 cherry tomatoes

ANCHOVY & OLIVE FILLING

50 g/1¾ oz canned anchovy fillets
  in olive oil

8 pimiento-stuffed green olives,
  finely chopped

2 large hard-boiled eggs,
  finely chopped

pepper

CRAB MAYONNAISE FILLING

170 g/6 oz canned crabmeat,
  drained

4 tbsp mayonnaise

1 tbsp chopped fresh
  flat-leaf parsley

salt and pepper

paprika, to garnish

BLACK OLIVE & CAPER FILLING

12 stoned black olives

3 tbsp capers

6 tbsp Aïoli (see page 12)

salt and pepper

1 If necessary, cut and discard a very thin slice from the stalk end of each tomato to make the bases flat and stable. Cut a thin slice from the smooth end of each cherry tomato and discard. Using a serrated knife or teaspoon, loosen the pulp and seeds of each and scoop out, discarding the flesh. Turn the scooped-out tomatoes upside down on kitchen paper and leave to drain for 5 minutes.

2 To make the anchovy and olive filling, drain the anchovies, reserving the olive oil for later, then chop finely and place in a bowl. Add the olives and hard-boiled eggs. Pour in a trickle of the reserved olive oil to moisten the mixture, then season with pepper. (Don't add salt to season as the anchovies are salty.) Mix well together.

3 To make the crab mayonnaise filling, place the crabmeat, mayonnaise and parsley in a bowl and mix well together. Season the filling to taste with salt and pepper. Sprinkle with paprika before serving.

4 To make the black olive and caper filling, place the olives and capers on kitchen paper to drain them well, then chop finely and place in a bowl. Add the Aïoli and mix well together. Season the filling to taste with salt and pepper.

5 Fill a piping bag fitted with a 2-cm/¾-inch plain nozzle with the filling of your choice and use to fill the hollow tomato shells. Store the cherry tomatoes in the refrigerator until ready to serve.

tomato & olive salad

serves six

2 tbsp sherry or red wine vinegar

5 tbsp olive oil

1 garlic clove, finely chopped

1 tsp paprika

4 tomatoes, peeled and diced

12 anchovy-stuffed or pimiento-
stuffed olives

½ cucumber, peeled and diced

2 shallots, finely chopped

1 tbsp pickled capers in brine,
drained

2–3 chicory heads, separated
into leaves

salt

COOK'S TIP

Although tomatoes are associated with Italian cooking, it was the Spanish who first brought this new ingredient from Peru to Europe in the sixteenth century and Spanish cooks were the first to develop recipes to use them.

1 First, make the dressing. Whisk the vinegar, olive oil, garlic and paprika together in a bowl. Season to taste with salt and reserve.

2 Place the tomatoes, olives, cucumber, shallots and capers in a separate bowl. Pour over the dressing and toss lightly.

3 Line 6 individual serving bowls with chicory leaves. Spoon an equal quantity of the salad into the centre of each and serve.

stuffed tomatoes with rice

serves four–eight

140 g/5 oz long-grain rice

140 g/5 oz black olives, stoned
and chopped

3 tbsp olive oil

4 beef or other large tomatoes,
halved

4 tbsp chopped fresh parsley

salt and pepper

VARIATION

This filling is also delicious in red
or yellow peppers. Halve and
deseed the peppers, then blanch
in lightly salted boiling water for
5 minutes. Drain well, refresh
under cold running water and
drain again. Peel and deseed
4 standard tomatoes and add the
chopped flesh to the rice and
olive mixture.

1 Bring a large saucepan of lightly salted water to the boil. Add the rice, return to the boil and stir once. Reduce the heat and cook for 10–15 minutes, or until only just tender. Drain well, rinse under cold running water and drain again. Line a large, shallow dish with kitchen paper, then spread out the rice on top for about 1 hour to dry.

2 Mix the rice, olives and olive oil together in a bowl and season well with pepper. You will probably not require any additional salt. Cover with clingfilm and leave to stand at room temperature for 8 hours or overnight.

3 Cut a slice off the tops of the tomatoes and, using a teaspoon, carefully scoop out and discard the seeds without piercing the shells. Scoop out the flesh, finely chop and add to the rice and olive mixture. Season the insides of the shells to taste with salt, then turn them upside down on kitchen paper and leave to drain for 1 hour.

4 Pat the insides of the tomato shells dry with kitchen paper, then divide the rice and olive mixture between them. Sprinkle with the parsley and serve.

garlic tomatoes

serves six

8 deep red tomatoes

3 fresh thyme sprigs, plus extra
   to garnish

12 garlic cloves, unpeeled

75 ml/2½ fl oz olive oil

salt and pepper

1 Preheat the oven to 220°C/425°F/
Gas Mark 7. Cut the tomatoes in
half lengthways and arrange, cut-side
up, in a single layer in a large,
ovenproof dish. Tuck the thyme sprigs
and garlic cloves between them.

2 Drizzle the olive oil all over the
tomatoes and season to taste
with pepper. Bake in the preheated
oven for 40–45 minutes, or until the
tomatoes are softened and beginning
to char slightly around the edges.

3 Remove and discard the thyme
sprigs. Season the tomatoes to
taste with salt and pepper, garnish
with the extra thyme sprigs and
serve hot or warm. Squeeze the pulp
from the garlic over the tomatoes at
the table.

COOK'S TIP

Sun-ripened tomatoes are perfect
for this dish as they have a much
fuller, sweeter flavour than
tomatoes ripened under glass.

courgettes with cheese & vinaigrette

serves six

550 g/1 lb 4 oz courgettes,
   sliced lengthways
6 tbsp olive oil
175 g/6 oz young Manchego or
   mozzarella cheese, diced
salt and pepper
fresh lemon balm leaves, to garnish
LEMON VINAIGRETTE
5 tbsp olive oil
4 tbsp lemon juice
1 tbsp clear honey
1 tsp finely grated lemon rind

COOK'S TIP

Manchego is probably Spain's
best-known cheese and has been
made in La Mancha since Roman
times. It is sold at different
stages of maturity; the fresh
cheese does not have the
peppery bite characteristic
of aged Manchego.

1 Preheat the oven to 200°C/
400°F/Gas Mark 6. Place the
courgettes in a roasting tin, pour over
the olive oil and season to taste with
salt and pepper. Toss well to coat.
Roast in the preheated oven, stirring
and tossing 2–3 times, for 30 minutes,
or until golden brown.

2 Meanwhile, make the lemon
vinaigrette. Whisk the olive oil,
lemon juice, honey and lemon rind
together in a bowl and season to taste
with salt and pepper.

3 Transfer the courgettes to a
serving dish and pour over the
vinaigrette. Toss gently and leave to
cool to room temperature. Just before
serving, sprinkle over the cheese and
garnish with lemon balm leaves.

courgette fritters with a dipping sauce

serves six–eight

450 g/1 lb baby courgettes

3 tbsp plain flour

1 tsp paprika

1 large egg

2 tbsp milk

sunflower oil, for shallow-frying

coarse sea salt

dipping sauce such as

Aïoli (see page 12), Fiery Tomato

    Salsa (see page 112) or the Pine

    Kernel Sauce (see below)

PINE KERNEL SAUCE

100 g/3½ oz pine kernels

1 garlic clove, peeled

3 tbsp Spanish extra virgin olive oil

1 tbsp lemon juice

3 tbsp water

1 tbsp chopped fresh

    flat-leaf parsley

salt and pepper

VARIATION

The exact same treatment can be applied to aubergines, while the sauce can be made with almonds in exactly the same way.

---

1 If you have chosen to serve the Pine Kernel Sauce with the courgette fritters, then make this first. Place the pine kernels and garlic in a food processor and process to form a purée. With the motor still running, gradually add the olive oil, lemon juice and water to form a smooth sauce. Stir in the parsley and season to taste with salt and pepper. Transfer to a serving bowl and reserve until required.

2 To prepare the courgettes, cut them on the diagonal into thin slices about 5 mm/¼ inch thick. Place the flour and paprika in a polythene bag and mix together. Beat the egg and milk together in a large bowl.

3 Add the courgette slices to the flour mixture and toss well together until coated. Shake off the excess flour. Heat the sunflower oil in a large, heavy-based frying pan to a depth of about 1 cm/½ inch. Dip the courgette slices, one at a time, into the egg mixture, then slip them into the hot oil. Fry the courgette slices, in batches in a single layer so that they do not overcrowd the frying pan, for 2 minutes, or until they are crisp and golden brown.

4 Using a slotted spoon, remove the courgette fritters from the frying pan and drain on kitchen paper. Continue until all the courgette slices have been fried.

5 Serve the courgette fritters piping hot, lightly sprinkled with sea salt. Accompany with a bowl of your chosen dipping sauce.

deep-fried green chillies

each 250-g/9-oz bag of chillies serves four–six

olive oil

sweet or hot fresh green chillies

sea salt

1 Heat 7.5 cm/3 inches of olive oil in a large, heavy-based saucepan until it reaches 190°C/375°F, or until a cube of bread turns brown in 30 seconds.

2 Rinse the chillies and pat them very dry with kitchen paper. Drop them in the hot oil for no longer than 20 seconds, or until they turn bright green and the skins blister.

3 Remove with a slotted spoon and drain well on crumpled kitchen paper. Sprinkle with sea salt and serve immediately.

VARIATION

For a more elaborate tapas, top a thin slice of bread with a fried egg, yolk-side up. Secure the egg to the bread by skewering the set white to the bread with a wooden cocktail stick with a fried chilli or pimiento de Padrón on it.

COOK'S TIP

Any sweet or hot chilli peppers can be quickly deep-fried, and the stubby pimientos de Padrón make an intriguing tapas when fried whole. You will find them in Spanish foodstores and some supermarkets sold in 250-g/ 9-oz bags. They have a fresh chilli taste, without much heat – except every bag seems to include one searingly hot chilli!

deep-fried cauliflower

serves four–six

1 cauliflower, cut into florets

1 egg

150 ml/5 fl oz milk

115 g/4 oz plain flour

vegetable oil, for deep-frying

salt

Tomato & Pepper Salsa (see page 7),
or Aïoli (see page 12), to serve

1 Bring a large saucepan of lightly salted water to the boil. Add the cauliflower florets, reduce the heat and simmer gently for 5 minutes. Drain well, refresh under cold running water and drain again.

COOK'S TIP

Fritters of every sort feature in traditional tapas bars throughout Spain. They may be served on their own or with a tasty sauce for dipping.

2 Beat the egg and milk together in a bowl until combined. Gradually whisk in the flour and 1 teaspoon salt.

3 Meanwhile, heat the vegetable oil for deep-frying to 180–190°C/ 350–375°F, or until a cube of bread browns in 30 seconds.

4 Dip the cauliflower florets in the batter, drain off the excess, then deep-fry, in batches if necessary, for 5 minutes, or until golden. Drain on kitchen paper, then serve immediately in warmed bowls with Tomato & Pepper Salsa or Aïoli.

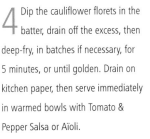

french beans with pine kernels

serves eight

2 tbsp Spanish olive oil

50 g/1¾ oz pine kernels

½–1 tsp paprika

450 g/1 lb French beans

1 small onion, finely chopped

1 garlic clove, finely chopped

juice of ½ lemon

salt and pepper

1 Heat the olive oil in a large, heavy-based frying pan. Add the pine kernels and fry for 1 minute, stirring constantly and shaking the pan, until light golden brown. Using a slotted spoon, remove the pine kernels from the frying pan, drain well on kitchen paper, then transfer to a bowl. Reserve the oil in the frying pan for later. Add the paprika, according to taste, to the pine kernels, stir together until coated, then reserve.

2 Top and tail the French beans and remove any strings if necessary. Place the beans in a saucepan, pour over boiling water, return to the boil and cook for 5 minutes, or until tender but still firm. Drain well in a colander.

3 Reheat the oil in the frying pan. Add the onion and fry for 5–10 minutes, or until softened and beginning to brown. Add the garlic and fry for a further 30 seconds.

4 Add the beans to the frying pan and cook for 2–3 minutes, tossing together with the onion until heated through. Season to taste with salt and pepper.

5 Turn the contents of the frying pan into a warmed serving dish, sprinkle over the lemon juice and toss together. Sprinkle over the reserved golden pine kernels and serve hot.

french beans with almonds

serves four–six

500 g/1 lb 2 oz French beans

55 g/2 oz butter

25 g/1 oz flaked almonds

2 tsp lemon juice

salt

1 Bring a saucepan of lightly salted water to the boil. Add the beans and leave to simmer for 8–10 minutes, or until just tender but still retaining a slight 'bite'.

2 Meanwhile, melt the butter in a heavy-based frying pan. Add the almonds and cook over a low heat, stirring frequently, for 3–5 minutes, or until golden. Stir in the lemon juice and season to taste with salt.

3 Drain the beans and add to the frying pan. Stir well to mix, then transfer to individual serving dishes and serve warm.

VARIATION

For a delicious variation to this dish, try substituting chopped, unsalted pistachio nuts for the almonds, and orange juice for the lemon juice.

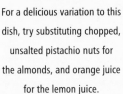

green beans in tomato sauce

serves six

25 g/1 oz butter

2 garlic cloves, finely chopped

2 spring onions, finely chopped

1 kg/2 lb 4 oz French beans, cut into
2.5-cm/1-inch lengths

700 g/1 lb 9 oz canned chopped
tomatoes

1 tbsp pine kernels

1 tbsp lemon juice

1 bay leaf

salt and pepper

1 Melt the butter in a large, heavy-based frying pan. Add the garlic and spring onions and cook over a medium heat, stirring occasionally, for 3–4 minutes. Add the beans and cook, stirring frequently, for a further 4 minutes.

VARIATION

This is also a delicious way to serve mangetout – there is no need to cut them into shorter lengths.

2 Add the tomatoes with their can juices, pine kernels, lemon juice and bay leaf and season to taste with salt and pepper. Reduce the heat and leave to simmer gently for 30 minutes, or until the beans are tender and the sauce is pulpy.

3 Remove and discard the bay leaf. Taste and adjust the seasoning if necessary. Transfer to warmed serving dishes and serve hot.

buttered cucumber

serves four

1 large cucumber, peeled and
    halved lengthways
55 g/2 oz butter
1 tbsp lemon juice
1 tbsp finely chopped fresh mint
salt and pepper

COOK'S TIP
You can serve this tapas with
forks or with wooden cocktail
sticks, depending on how
dextrous your guests are.

1 Scoop out the seeds from the
cucumber using a teaspoon.
Cut each cucumber half into 2-cm/
¾-inch slices and place in a colander,
sprinkling each layer with salt. Leave to
drain for 30 minutes, then rinse under
cold running water and drain well. Pat
dry with kitchen paper.

2 Melt the butter in a large,
heavy-based frying pan. Add
the cucumber and cook over a
medium heat, stirring constantly, for
3–5 minutes, or until thoroughly hot.

3 Stir in the lemon juice and mint
and season to taste with pepper.
Transfer to warmed serving dishes and
serve hot.

moorish courgette salad

serves four–six

500 g/18 oz small courgettes

about 4 tbsp olive oil

1 large garlic clove, halved

55 g/2 oz pine kernels

55 g/2 oz raisins

3 tbsp finely chopped fresh mint
leaves (not spearmint
or peppermint)

about 2 tbsp lemon juice, or to taste

salt and pepper

VARIATION

For a more robust flavour, chop 4 drained anchovy fillets in oil and add in Step 2.

COOK'S TIP

This salad is best made with young, tender courgettes no more than 2.5 cm/1 inch thick. If using older, larger courgettes, cut them in half or quarters lengthways first, then slice thinly.

1 Slice the courgettes thinly (see Cook's Tip). Heat the oil in a large frying pan over a medium heat. Add the garlic and let it fry until golden to flavour the oil, then remove and discard. Add the courgettes and fry, stirring, until just tender. Immediately remove from the frying pan and transfer to a large serving bowl.

2 Add the pine kernels, raisins, mint, lemon juice and salt and pepper to taste, and stir. Taste, and add more olive oil, lemon juice and seasoning, if necessary.

3 Leave the salad to cool completely. Cover and chill for at least 3½ hours. Remove from the refrigerator 10 minutes before serving.

orange & fennel salad

serves four

4 large, juicy oranges

1 large fennel bulb, very
   thinly sliced

1 mild white onion, finely sliced

2 tbsp extra virgin olive oil

12 plump black olives, stoned and
   thinly sliced

1 fresh red chilli, deseeded and very
   thinly sliced (optional)

finely chopped fresh parsley

French bread, to serve

1 Finely grate the rind from the oranges into a bowl and reserve. Using a small, serrated knife, remove all the white pith from the oranges, working over a bowl to catch the juices. Cut the oranges horizontally into thin slices.

2 Toss the orange slices with the fennel and onion slices. Whisk the olive oil into the reserved orange juice, then spoon over the oranges. Sprinkle the olive slices over the top, add the chilli, if using, then sprinkle with the orange rind and parsley. Serve with slices of French bread.

VARIATION

For a more substantial meal, add soaked and cooked salt cod (see page 122). Garnet-red blood oranges look stunning. Juicy dark grapes make an interesting alternative to the olives.

pimientos with curd cheese & fresh herbs

makes seven–eight

185 g/6½ oz canned or bottled
  whole pimientos del piquillo
  (see page 160)

salt and pepper

fresh herb sprigs, to garnish

CURD CHEESE & HERB FILLING

225 g/8 oz curd cheese

1 tsp lemon juice

1 garlic clove, crushed

4 tbsp chopped fresh
  flat-leaf parsley

1 tbsp chopped fresh mint

1 tbsp chopped fresh oregano

TUNA MAYONNAISE FILLING

200 g/7 oz canned tuna in
  olive oil, drained

5 tbsp mayonnaise

2 tsp lemon juice

2 tbsp chopped fresh
  flat-leaf parsley

GOAT'S CHEESE & OLIVE FILLING

50 g/1¾ oz stoned black olives,
  finely chopped

200 g/7 oz soft goat's cheese

1 garlic clove, crushed

1 There is a choice of fillings provided in this recipe – the final decision is yours. Lift the peppers from the jar, reserving the oil for later use.

2 To make the curd cheese and herb filling, place the curd cheese in a bowl and add the lemon juice, garlic, parsley, mint and oregano. Mix together well. Season to taste with salt and pepper.

3 To make the tuna and mayonnaise filling, place the tuna in a bowl and add the mayonnaise, lemon juice and parsley. Add 1 tablespoon of the reserved oil from the jar of pimientos and mix well. Season to taste with salt and pepper.

4 To make the goat's cheese and olive filling, place the olives in a bowl and add the goat's cheese, garlic and 1 tablespoon of the reserved oil from the jar of pimientos. Mix well together. Season to taste with salt and pepper.

5 Using a teaspoon, heap the filling of your choice into each pimiento. Leave to chill in the refrigerator for at least 2 hours until firm.

6 To serve the pimientos, arrange them on a serving plate and, if necessary, wipe with kitchen paper to remove any of the filling that has spread over the skins. Garnish with herb sprigs and serve.

asparagus & fried eggs

500 g/1 lb 2 oz asparagus spears

2 tbsp olive oil

6 eggs

1 Trim and discard the coarse, woody ends of the asparagus spears. Make sure all the stems are about the same length, then tie them together loosely with clean kitchen string. If you have an asparagus steamer, you don't need to tie the stems together – just place them in the basket.

2 Bring a tall saucepan of lightly salted water to the boil. Add the asparagus, making sure that the tips are protruding above the water, reduce the heat and leave to simmer for 10–15 minutes, or until tender. Test by piercing a stem just above the water level with the point of a sharp knife.

COOK'S TIP

The asparagus spears are eaten with the fingers and dipped in the egg yolk. The egg white is not eaten.

3 Meanwhile, heat a little of the olive oil in a large, heavy-based frying pan. Add 2 eggs, if there is enough room, and fry over a medium–low heat until the whites are just set and the yolks are still runny. Transfer to warmed serving plates and cook the remaining eggs in the same way.

4 Drain the asparagus and divide the spears between the plates. Serve immediately.

VARIATION

You can also serve the asparagus with lightly boiled eggs for dipping in the same way.

roasted asparagus with serrano ham

makes twelve

2 tbsp Spanish olive oil

6 slices serrano ham

12 asparagus spears

pepper

Aïoli (see page 12), to serve

1 Preheat the oven to 200°C/
400°F/Gas Mark 6. Place half the
olive oil in a roasting tin that will hold
the asparagus spears in a single layer
and swirl it around so that it covers
the base. Cut each slice of serrano ham
in half lengthways.

2 Trim and discard the coarse,
woody ends of the asparagus
spears, then wrap a slice of ham
around the stem end of each spear.
Place the wrapped spears in the
prepared roasting tin and lightly brush
with the remaining olive oil. Season
the asparagus with pepper.

3 Roast the asparagus spears in the
preheated oven for 10 minutes,
depending on the thickness of the
asparagus, until tender but still firm.
Do not overcook the asparagus spears
as it is important that they are still
firm, so that you can pick them up with
your fingers.

4 Serve the roasted asparagus
piping hot, accompanied by a
bowl of Aïoli for dipping.

chargrilled leeks

serves four

8 baby leeks

2 tbsp olive oil, plus extra
for brushing

2 tbsp white wine vinegar

2 tbsp snipped fresh chives

2 tbsp chopped fresh parsley

1 tsp Dijon mustard

salt and pepper

fresh parsley sprigs, to garnish

1 Trim the leeks and halve lengthways. Rinse well to remove any grit and pat dry with kitchen paper.

2 Heat a griddle pan and brush with olive oil. Add the leeks and cook over a medium–high heat, turning occasionally, for 5 minutes. Transfer to a shallow dish.

COOK'S TIP

If you don't have a griddle pan, brush the leeks with olive oil and cook under a preheated grill, turning occasionally and brushing with more oil.

3 Meanwhile, whisk the olive oil, vinegar, chives, parsley and mustard together in a bowl and season to taste with salt and pepper. Pour over the leeks, turning to coat. Cover with clingfilm and leave to marinate at room temperature, turning occasionally, for 30 minutes.

4 Divide the leeks between individual serving plates, garnish with parsley sprigs and serve.

roasted peppers with honey & almonds

serves six

8 red peppers, quartered and
   deseeded

4 tbsp olive oil

2 garlic cloves, thinly sliced

25 g/1 oz flaked almonds

2 tbsp clear honey

2 tbsp sherry vinegar

2 tbsp chopped fresh parsley

salt and pepper

1 Preheat the grill to high. Place the peppers, skin-side up, in a single layer on a baking sheet. Cook under the hot grill for 8–10 minutes, or until the skins have blistered and blackened. Using tongs, transfer to a polythene bag, tie the top and leave to cool.

2 When the peppers are cool enough to handle, peel off the skin with your fingers or a knife and discard it. Chop the flesh into bite-sized pieces and place in a bowl.

3 Heat the olive oil in a large, heavy-based frying pan. Add the garlic and cook over a low heat, stirring frequently, for 4 minutes, or until golden. Stir in the almonds, honey and vinegar, then pour the mixture over the pepper quarters. Add the parsley, season to taste with salt and pepper and toss well.

4 Leave to cool to room temperature before transferring to serving dishes. The peppers may also be covered and stored in the refrigerator, but should be returned to room temperature for serving.

roasted pepper salad

serves eight

3 red peppers

3 yellow peppers

5 tbsp Spanish extra virgin olive oil

2 tbsp dry sherry vinegar or
   lemon juice

2 garlic cloves, crushed

pinch of sugar

1 tbsp capers

8 small black Spanish olives

salt and pepper

2 tbsp chopped fresh marjoram,
   plus extra sprigs to garnish

1 Preheat the grill. Place all the peppers on a wire rack or grill pan and cook under the hot grill for 10 minutes, or until their skins have blackened and blistered all over, turning them frequently.

2 Remove the roasted peppers from the heat, place them in a bowl and immediately cover tightly with a clean, damp tea towel.

3 Alternatively, place the peppers in a polythene bag. You will find that the steam helps to soften the skins and makes it easier to remove them. Leave the peppers for about 15 minutes, or until they are cool enough to handle.

4 Holding 1 pepper at a time over a clean bowl, use a sharp knife to make a small hole in the base and gently squeeze out the juices and reserve them. Still holding the pepper over the bowl, carefully peel off the skin with your fingers or a knife and discard it. Cut the peppers in half and remove the stem, core and seeds, then cut each pepper into neat thin strips. Arrange the pepper strips attractively on a serving dish.

5 Add the olive oil, sherry vinegar, garlic, sugar and salt and pepper to taste to the reserved pepper juices. Whisk together until combined, then drizzle the dressing over the salad.

6 Sprinkle the capers, olives and chopped marjoram over the salad, garnish with marjoram sprigs and serve at room temperature.

artichoke hearts & asparagus

serves four–six

450 g/1 lb asparagus spears

400 g/14 oz canned artichoke
   hearts, drained and rinsed

2 tbsp freshly squeezed orange juice

½ tsp finely grated orange rind

2 tbsp walnut oil

1 tsp Dijon mustard

salad leaves, to serve

salt and pepper

1 Trim and discard the coarse, woody ends of the asparagus spears. Make sure all the stems are about the same length, then tie them together loosely with clean kitchen string. If you have an asparagus steamer, you don't need to tie the stems together — just place them in the basket.

2 Bring a tall saucepan of lightly salted water to the boil. Add the asparagus, making sure that the tips are protruding above the water, reduce the heat and leave to simmer for 10–15 minutes, or until tender. Test by piercing a stem just above the water level with the point of a sharp knife. Drain, refresh under cold running water and drain again.

3 Cut the asparagus spears into 2.5-cm/1-inch pieces, keeping the tips intact. Cut the artichoke hearts into small wedges and combine with the asparagus in a bowl.

4 Whisk the orange juice, orange rind, walnut oil and mustard together in a bowl and season to taste with salt and pepper. If serving immediately, pour the dressing over the artichoke hearts and asparagus and toss lightly.

5 Arrange the salad leaves in individual serving dishes and top with the artichoke and asparagus mixture. Serve immediately. Alternatively, store the salad, covered, in the refrigerator and add the dressing just before serving.

melon, chorizo & artichoke salad

serves eight

12 small globe artichokes

juice of ½ lemon

2 tbsp Spanish olive oil

1 small orange-fleshed melon,
   such as cantaloupe

200 g/7 oz chorizo sausage,
   outer casing removed

fresh tarragon or flat-leaf parsley
   sprigs, to garnish

DRESSING

3 tbsp Spanish extra virgin olive oil

1 tbsp red wine vinegar

1 tsp prepared mustard

1 tbsp chopped fresh tarragon

salt and pepper

VARIATION

You could use serrano ham, cut
in one thick piece rather than
sliced, instead of the chorizo.

1 To prepare the artichokes, cut off the stalks. With your hands, break off the toughest outer leaves at the base until the tender inside leaves are visible. Using a pair of scissors, cut the spiky tips off the leaves. Using a sharp knife, pare the dark green skin from the base and down the stem. As you prepare them, brush the cut surfaces of the artichokes with lemon juice to prevent discoloration. Alternatively, you could fill a bowl with cold water to which you have added a little lemon juice, and immerse the artichokes in the acidulated water to stop discolouration. Carefully remove the choke (the mass of silky hairs) by pulling it out with your fingers or by scooping it out with a spoon. It is very important to remove all the choke as the little barbs, if eaten, can irritate the throat. However, if you are using very young artichokes, you do not need to worry about removing the choke and you can include the stalk too, well scraped, as it will be quite tender. Cut the artichokes into quarters and brush them again with lemon juice.

2 Heat the olive oil in a large, heavy-based frying pan. Add the prepared artichokes and fry, stirring frequently, for 5 minutes, or until the artichoke leaves are golden brown. Remove from the frying pan, transfer to a large serving bowl and leave to cool.

3 To prepare the melon, cut in half and scoop out the seeds with a spoon. Cut the flesh into bite-sized cubes. Add to the cooled artichokes. Cut the chorizo into bite-sized chunks and add to the melon and artichokes.

4 To make the dressing, place all the ingredients in a small bowl and whisk together. Just before serving, pour the dressing over the prepared salad ingredients and toss together. Serve the salad garnished with tarragon or parsley sprigs.

sautéed garlic mushrooms

serves six

450 g/1 lb button mushrooms

5 tbsp Spanish olive oil

2 garlic cloves, finely chopped

lemon juice

4 tbsp chopped fresh parsley

salt and pepper

lemon wedges, to garnish

crusty bread, to serve

1 Wipe or brush clean the mushrooms, then trim off the stalks close to the caps. Cut any large mushrooms in half or into quarters. Heat the olive oil in a large, heavy-based frying pan. Add the garlic and fry for 30 seconds–1 minute, or until lightly browned. Add the mushrooms and sauté over a high heat, stirring frequently, until the mushrooms have absorbed all the oil in the frying pan.

2 Reduce the heat to low. When the juices have come out of the mushrooms, increase the heat again and sauté for 4–5 minutes, stirring frequently, until the juices have almost evaporated. Add a squeeze of lemon juice and season to taste with salt and pepper. Stir in the parsley and cook for a further 1 minute.

3 Transfer the sautéed mushrooms to a warmed serving dish, garnish with lemon wedges and serve piping hot or warm. Accompany with crusty bread for mopping up the juices.

VARIATION

Wild mushrooms such as boletus or chanterelles can be used in place of cultivated mushrooms. Courgettes may also be prepared in the same way, with a finely chopped small onion fried in the oil until lightly browned before adding the garlic.

chilli mushrooms

serves six–eight

55 g/2 oz butter

5 tbsp olive oil

1 kg/2 lb 4 oz button mushrooms

4 fat garlic cloves, finely chopped

1 fresh red chilli, deseeded and
   finely chopped

1 tbsp lemon juice

salt and pepper

fresh parsley sprigs, to garnish

1 Heat the butter with the olive oil in a large, heavy-based frying pan. When the butter has melted, add the mushrooms, garlic and chilli and cook over a medium–low heat, stirring frequently, for 5 minutes.

2 Stir in the lemon juice and season to taste with salt and pepper.

3 Transfer to warmed serving dishes and serve immediately, garnished with parsley sprigs.

VARIATION

For a spicier dish, increase the
quantity of fresh chillies or
season with salt and cayenne,
rather than ground black pepper.

stuffed mushrooms

serves six

175 g/6 oz butter

4 garlic cloves, finely chopped

6 large open mushrooms,
   stems removed

55 g/2 oz fresh white breadcrumbs

1 tbsp chopped fresh thyme

1 egg, lightly beaten

salt and pepper

COOK'S TIP

For a more substantial tapas,
serve these mushrooms on toast.
Stamp out rounds of bread with
a biscuit cutter, then toast on
both sides. Spread with butter or
more garlic butter, then top each
round with a stuffed mushroom.

1 Preheat the oven to 180°C/
350°F/Gas Mark 4. Cream the
butter in a bowl until softened, then
beat in the garlic. Divide two-thirds
of the garlic butter between the
mushroom caps and arrange them,
cup-side up, on a baking sheet.

2 Melt the remaining garlic butter in
a heavy-based or non-stick frying
pan. Add the breadcrumbs and cook
over a low heat, stirring frequently,
until golden. Remove from the heat
and tip into a bowl. Stir in the thyme
and season to taste with salt and
pepper. Stir in the beaten egg until
thoroughly combined.

3 Divide the breadcrumb mixture
between the mushroom caps
and bake in the preheated oven for
15 minutes, or until the stuffing is
golden brown and the mushrooms
are tender. Serve hot or warm.

stuffed peppers

makes six

6 tbsp olive oil, plus a little extra for
    rubbing on peppers
2 onions, finely chopped
2 garlic cloves, crushed
140 g/5 oz Spanish short-grain rice
55 g/2 oz raisins
55 g/2 oz pine kernels
40 g/1½ oz fresh parsley,
    finely chopped
1 tbsp tomato purée dissolved in
    700 ml/1¼ pints hot water
salt and pepper
4–6 red, green or yellow peppers
    (or a mix of colours), or 6 of
    the long, Mediterranean variety

COOK'S TIP

If you are using the pointed,
Mediterranean variety of pepper,
a melon baller, teaspoon or small
paring knife makes it easier to
remove all the seeds.

1 Preheat the oven to 200°C/
400°F/Gas Mark 6. Heat the oil
in a shallow, heavy-based flameproof
casserole. Add the onions and fry for
3 minutes. Add the garlic and fry for
a further 2 minutes, or until the onion
is soft but not brown.

2 Stir in the rice, raisins and pine
kernels until all are coated in the
oil, then add half the parsley and salt
and pepper to taste. Stir in the tomato
purée and bring to the boil. Reduce the
heat and leave to simmer, uncovered,
shaking the casserole frequently, for
20 minutes or until the rice is tender,
the liquid is absorbed and small holes
appear on the surface. Watch carefully
because the raisins can catch and burn.
Stir in the remaining parsley, then leave
to cool slightly.

3 While the rice is simmering,
cut the top off each pepper and
reserve. Remove the core and seeds
from each pepper (see Cook's Tip).

4 Divide the stuffing equally
between the peppers. Use
wooden cocktail sticks to secure the
tops back in place. Lightly rub each
pepper with olive oil and arrange in
a single layer in a baking dish. Bake in
the preheated oven for 30 minutes, or
until the peppers are tender. Serve hot
or leave to cool to room temperature.

red peppers with vinegar & capers

serves six

1 tbsp capers

4 tbsp olive oil

1 kg/2 lb 4 oz red peppers, halved,
deseeded and cut into strips

4 garlic cloves, finely chopped

2 tbsp sherry vinegar

salt and pepper

COOK'S TIP

Capers preserved in salt
are best for this dish; those
preserved in vinegar are less
suitable. If you can find them,
try capers preserved in olive
oil and use some of the oil
from the jar for cooking.

1 If using salted capers, brush off most of the salt with your fingers. If using pickled capers in vinegar, drain well and rinse thoroughly.

2 Heat the olive oil in a heavy-based frying pan. Add the pepper strips and cook over a medium heat, stirring frequently, for 10 minutes, or until softened and charred around the edges. Add the capers and garlic and cook for a further 2–3 minutes.

3 Stir in the vinegar and season to taste with salt and pepper – season sparingly with salt if using salted capers. Cook for 1–2 minutes, then remove from the heat. Serve immediately or leave to cool, cover and chill before serving.

roasted peppers with fiery cheese

serves six

1 red pepper, halved and
  deseeded
1 orange pepper, halved and
  deseeded
1 yellow pepper, halved and
  deseeded
115 g/4 oz Afuega'l Pitu cheese or
  other hot spiced cheese, diced
1 tbsp clear honey
1 tbsp sherry vinegar
salt and pepper

COOK'S TIP

Afuega'l Pitu means 'fire in the
belly' and this is an apt
description for the chilli-
flavoured cheese from Asturias.
If it is not available, you could
use Hungarian Liptauer.
Liptauer is spiced with paprika
rather than chillies, but is still
astonishingly spicy.

1 Preheat the grill to high. Place the peppers, skin-side up, in a single layer on a baking sheet. Cook under the hot grill for 8–10 minutes, or until the skins have blistered and blackened. Using tongs, transfer to a polythene bag, tie the top and leave to cool.

2 When the peppers are cool enough to handle, peel off the skin with your fingers or a knife and discard it. Place on a serving plate and sprinkle over the cheese.

3 Whisk the honey and vinegar together in a bowl and season to taste with salt and pepper. Pour the dressing over the peppers, cover and leave to chill until required.

pickled stuffed peppers

serves six

200 g/7 oz Cuajada cheese,
  Queso del Tietar or other goat's
  milk cheese
400 g/14 oz pickled peppers or
  pimientos del piquillo, drained
1 tbsp finely chopped fresh dill
salt and pepper

1 Cut the cheese into pieces about 1 cm/½ inch long. Slit the sides of the peppers and deseed, if you like. Stuff the peppers with the cheese.

2 Arrange the stuffed peppers on serving plates, sprinkle with the dill and season to taste with salt and pepper. Cover and chill until required.

COOK'S TIP

Pimientos del piquillo are available from delicatessens and some large supermarkets, but you can use any type of pickled pepper for this tapas. You can also make a spicier version with pickled chillies.

white bean vinaigrette

serves four–six

400 g/14 oz canned butter beans

3 celery stalks, chopped

1 gherkin, finely chopped

150 ml/5 fl oz olive oil

4 tbsp white wine vinegar

1 garlic clove, finely chopped

2 tsp Dijon mustard

1 tbsp chopped fresh parsley

pinch of sugar

salt and pepper

snipped fresh chives, to garnish

1 Drain the beans, rinse well under cold running water and drain again. Place the beans, celery and gherkin in a bowl.

2 Whisk the olive oil, vinegar, garlic, mustard, parsley and sugar together in a bowl and season to taste with salt and pepper.

3 Pour the vinaigrette over the bean mixture and toss well. Transfer to a serving dish, sprinkle with the chives and serve at room temperature or cover and leave to chill before serving.

VARIATION

You can also make this dish with other types of white beans, such as haricot, navy or cannellini.

empanadillas

serves six–eight

2 tbsp olive oil, plus extra
  for brushing
500 g/1 lb 2 oz fresh spinach leaves
2 garlic cloves, finely chopped
8 canned anchovy fillets in oil,
  drained and chopped
2 tbsp raisins, soaked in hot water
  for 10 minutes
40 g/1½ oz pine kernels
450 g/1 lb puff pastry, thawed
  if frozen
plain flour, for dusting
1 egg, lightly beaten
salt and pepper

COOK'S TIP

These little pastries originated in
Galicia but are now made all
over Spain and are extremely
popular in South America, too.

1 Preheat the oven to 180°C/
350°F/Gas Mark 4. Lightly brush
1–2 baking sheets with olive oil.

2 Trim and discard any tough stalks
from the spinach and finely chop
the leaves.

3 Heat the olive oil in a large
saucepan. Add the chopped
spinach, cover and cook over a low
heat, gently shaking the saucepan
occasionally, for 3 minutes. Stir in
the garlic and anchovies and cook,
uncovered, for a further 1 minute.
Remove the saucepan from the heat.

4 Drain the raisins and chop, then
stir them into the spinach mixture
with the pine kernels and salt and
pepper to taste. Leave to cool.

5 Roll out the pastry on a lightly
floured work surface to a round
about 3 mm/⅛ inch thick. Stamp out
rounds using a 7.5-cm/3-inch biscuit
cutter. Re-roll the trimmings and stamp
out more rounds.

6 Place 1–2 heaped teaspoonfuls
of the spinach filling onto each
pastry round. Brush the edges with
water and fold over to make half
moons. Press together well to seal.
Place the empanadillas on the baking
sheets, brush with beaten egg to glaze
and bake in the preheated oven for
15 minutes, or until golden brown.
Serve warm.

bandilleras

serves eight–ten

1 tbsp white wine vinegar

4 garlic cloves, finely chopped

1 fresh red chilli, deseeded and
  finely chopped

1 tbsp sweet paprika

4 tbsp olive oil

3 skinless, boneless chicken breasts,
  cut into 2.5-cm/1-inch cubes

1 avocado

3 tbsp lemon juice

115 g/4 oz San Simon or other
  smoked cheese, diced

8–10 black olives, stoned

8–10 cherry tomatoes

85 g/3 oz Manchego or Cheddar
  cheese, cubed

8–10 pimiento-stuffed green olives

½ cantaloupe melon, deseeded

5–6 slices serrano ham

PICADA

4 garlic cloves, finely chopped

6 tbsp chopped fresh parsley

6 tbsp pickled cucumber,
  finely chopped

150 ml/5 fl oz olive oil

1 Mix the vinegar, garlic, chilli, paprika and olive oil together in a bowl. Add the chicken, stir well to coat, then cover and leave to marinate in the refrigerator for at least 2 hours or preferably overnight.

2 Heat a large, heavy-based frying pan. Tip the chicken mixture into the pan and cook over a low heat, stirring frequently, for 10–15 minutes, or until cooked through. Remove from the heat and leave to cool to room temperature, then spear the chicken pieces with wooden cocktail sticks.

3 Peel and stone the avocado and cut into bite-sized cubes. Toss in the lemon juice, then thread onto wooden cocktail sticks with the smoked cheese. Thread the black olives, tomatoes, Manchego or Cheddar cheese and stuffed olives onto wooden cocktail sticks.

4 Scoop out 20 balls from the melon with a melon baller or teaspoon. Cut the ham into 20 strips and wrap around the melon balls. Thread the melon balls in pairs onto wooden cocktail sticks.

5 To make the Picada, mix all the ingredients together in a bowl until thoroughly combined into a fairly thick paste. Arrange all the filled cocktail sticks – bandilleras – on a large serving platter and serve with bowls of Picada.

Olives & Nuts

Spanish cooking is famous for its love of almonds and olives, so over the next few pages you will find a selection of recipes that are dedicated to these two essential ingredients.

If you're in the habit of inviting friends round for impromptu gatherings, keeping a jar or two of Marinated Olives (see page 84) in the storecupboard is a great way of having something tastier than shop-bought crisps and dips. The recipe for Salted Almonds (see page 89) is another famous nibble to serve with drinks, but it can be made equally well with other nuts — try walnut halves, pistachios, peanuts or cashews for a change.

marinated olives

fills a 500-ml/18-fl oz preserving jar

175 g/6 oz green pimiento-stuffed
   Spanish olives in brine, rinsed

175 g/6 oz black Spanish olives
   in brine, rinsed

55 g/2 oz grilled and peeled pepper
   (see page 213), thinly sliced

2 thin lemon slices

2 fresh thyme sprigs

1 bay leaf

1 dried red chilli

½ tsp fennel seeds

½ tsp coriander seeds,
   lightly cracked

extra virgin olive oil

COOK'S TIP

Do not add sliced garlic to an
oil marinade, because of the
possibility of botulism infection.
If you want a garlic flavour,
use a commercially prepared
garlic-flavoured olive oil instead.
If you store the marinade in the
refrigerator, the oil will become
cloudy, but it clears again as it
returns to room temperature.

1 Place the olives, pepper strips,
lemon slices, thyme, bay leaf,
chilli, fennel and coriander seeds in a
500-ml/18-fl oz preserving jar, making
sure the ingredients are well mixed.
Pour over enough olive oil to cover.

2 Seal the jar and leave at
room temperature for at least
2 weeks before using.

olives with orange & lemon

serves four–six

2 tsp fennel seeds

2 tsp cumin seeds

225 g/8 oz green olives

225 g/8 oz black olives

2 tsp grated orange rind

2 tsp grated lemon rind

3 shallots, finely chopped

pinch of ground cinnamon

4 tbsp white wine vinegar

5 tbsp olive oil

2 tbsp orange juice

1 tbsp chopped fresh mint

1 tbsp chopped fresh parsley

COOK'S TIP

For an authentic flavour, look for Spanish varieties of olive, such as arbequines, gordas del rey, manzanilla or perlas from Aragon.

1 Dry-fry the fennel seeds and cumin seeds in a small, heavy-based frying pan, shaking the pan frequently, until they begin to pop and give off their aroma. Remove the frying pan from the heat and leave to cool.

2 Place the olives, orange and lemon rind, shallots, cinnamon and toasted seeds in a bowl.

3 Whisk the vinegar, olive oil, orange juice, mint and parsley together in a bowl and pour over the olives. Toss well, cover and leave to chill for 1–2 days before serving.

olives wrapped with anchovies

makes twelve

12 anchovy fillets in oil, drained

24 pimiento-stuffed green olives
in oil, drained

1 Using a sharp knife, halve each
anchovy fillet lengthways.

2 Wrap a half fillet around the
middle of each olive, overlapping
the ends, and secure with a wooden
cocktail stick. Repeat with another olive
and anchovy fillet half and slide onto
the cocktail stick. Continue until
all the ingredients are used. Serve
immediately or cover until required.

VARIATION

Instead of using pimiento-stuffed
olives, stuff stoned green or
black olives with a blanched
almond sliver. Proceed with the
recipe as above.

spicy cracked marinated olives

serves eight

450 g/1 lb canned or bottled
    unstoned large green
    olives, drained

4 garlic cloves, peeled

2 tsp coriander seeds

1 small lemon

4 fresh thyme sprigs

4 feathery stalks of fennel

2 small fresh red chillies (optional)

Spanish extra virgin olive oil

pepper

1 To allow the flavours of the marinade to penetrate the olives, place them on a chopping board and, using a rolling pin, bash them lightly so that they crack slightly. Alternatively, use a sharp knife to cut a lengthways slit in each olive as far as the stone. Using the flat side of a broad knife, lightly crush each garlic clove. Using a pestle and mortar, crack the coriander seeds. Cut the lemon, with its rind, into small chunks.

2 Place the olives, garlic, coriander seeds, lemon chunks, thyme sprigs, fennel and chillies, if using, in a large bowl and toss together. Season to taste with pepper, but you should not need to add salt as canned or bottled olives are usually salty enough. Pack the ingredients tightly into a glass jar with a lid. Pour in enough olive oil to cover the olives, then seal the jar tightly.

3 Leave the olives at room temperature for 24 hours, then marinate in the refrigerator for at least 1 week but preferably 2 weeks before serving. From time to time, gently give the jar a shake to re-mix the ingredients. Return the olives to room temperature and remove from the oil to serve. Provide wooden cocktail sticks for spearing the olives.

paprika-spiced almonds

makes 500 g/1 lb 2 oz; serves four–six

1½ tbsp coarse sea salt

½ tsp smoked sweet Spanish paprika, or hot paprika, to taste

500 g/1 lb 2 oz blanched almonds

extra virgin olive oil

COOK'S TIP

It is best, and more economical, to buy unblanched almonds and blanch them as and when required, because they begin to dry out as soon as the thin, brown skin is removed. Put the unblanched almonds in a heatproof bowl. Pour over boiling water and leave to stand for 1 minute. Drain well, then pat dry and slip off the skins.

1 Preheat the oven to 200°C/400°F/Gas Mark 6. Place the sea salt and paprika in a mortar and grind with the pestle to a fine powder. Alternatively, use a mini spice blender (the amount is too small to process in a full-size processor).

2 Place the almonds on a baking sheet and toast in the preheated oven for 8–10 minutes, stirring occasionally, until golden and giving off a toasted aroma. Watch after 7 minutes because they burn quickly. Pour into a heatproof bowl.

3 Drizzle over 1 tablespoon of olive oil and stir to ensure all the nuts are lightly and evenly coated. Add extra oil, if necessary. Sprinkle with the salt and paprika mixture and stir again. Transfer to a small bowl and serve at room temperature.

salted almonds

serves six–eight

225 g/8 oz whole almonds, in their
  skins or blanched (see method)
4 tbsp Spanish olive oil
coarse sea salt
1 tsp paprika or ground cumin
  (optional)

1 Preheat the oven to 180°C/
350°F/Gas Mark 4. Fresh almonds
in their skins are superior in taste, but
blanched almonds are much more
convenient. If the almonds are not
blanched, place them in a large bowl,
cover with boiling water for 3–4
minutes, then plunge them into cold
water for 1 minute. Drain them well in
a sieve, then slide off the skins
between your fingers. Dry the almonds
well on kitchen paper.

2 Place the olive oil in a roasting tin
and swirl it around so that it
covers the base. Add the almonds and
toss them in the tin so that they are
evenly coated in the oil, then spread
them out in a single layer.

3 Roast the almonds in the
preheated oven for 20 minutes,
or until they are light golden brown,
tossing several times during the
cooking. Drain the almonds on kitchen
paper, then transfer them to a bowl.

4 While the almonds are still warm,
sprinkle with plenty of sea salt
and paprika, if using, and toss together
to coat. Serve the almonds warm or
cold. The almonds are at their best
when served freshly cooked, so, if
possible, cook them on the day that
you plan to eat them. However, they
can be stored in an airtight container
for up to 3 days.

Eggs & Cheese

Egg-based dishes feature in all tapas menus, and you will find recipes for such favourites as Spanish Tortilla (see page 100), full of flavour as well as very common ingredients, and Devilled Eggs (see page 96). Other tortilla recipes use spinach or chorizo for variety, while the Oven-baked Tortilla (see page 98), served on cocktail sticks in the bars of Madrid, makes a great lighter tapas dish.

There is a wide range of cheeses, and cheese dishes, in Spain, but it can be difficult to buy some of the more exotic types in other countries. For this reason, alternatives are suggested where the local cheese is likely to be unavailable.

basque scrambled eggs

serves four–six

3–4 tbsp olive oil

1 large onion, finely chopped

1 large red pepper, deseeded
and chopped

1 large green pepper, deseeded
and chopped

2 large tomatoes, peeled, deseeded
(see page 167) and chopped

55 g/2 oz chorizo sausage, sliced
thinly, outer casing removed,
if preferred

35 g/1¼ oz butter

10 large eggs, lightly beaten

salt and pepper

4–6 thick slices country-style bread,
toasted, to serve

1 Heat 2 tablespoons of olive oil in a large, heavy-based frying pan over a medium heat. Add the onion and peppers and cook for 5 minutes, or until the vegetables are softened but not browned. Add the tomatoes and heat through. Transfer to a heatproof plate and keep warm in a preheated low oven.

2 Add another tablespoon of oil to the frying pan. Add the chorizo and cook for 30 seconds, just to warm through and flavour the oil. Add the sausage to the reserved vegetables.

3 Add a little extra olive oil, if necessary, to bring it back to 2 tablespoons. Add the butter and allow to melt. Season the eggs with salt and pepper, then add to the pan and scramble until cooked to the desired degree of firmness. Return the vegetables to the pan and stir through. Serve immediately with hot toast.

basque eggs with peppers

serves six

2 red peppers, halved
and deseeded

6 hard-boiled eggs, cooled, shelled
and sliced

2 tbsp white wine vinegar

5 tbsp olive oil

1 shallot, finely chopped

2 tsp chopped fresh dill

pinch of sugar

salt and pepper

VARIATION

For extra colour, use one red and
one orange or yellow pepper.
Don't use green peppers, as they
are too sharp in flavour.

1 Bring a saucepan of water to the
boil. Add the peppers and blanch
for 5 minutes. Drain, refresh under cold
running water and drain well again.
Pat dry with kitchen paper and cut into
thin strips.

2 Arrange the slices of egg on
serving plates and sprinkle over
the pepper strips. Alternatively, make
a lattice pattern with the pepper strips.

3 Whisk the vinegar, olive oil,
shallot, dill and sugar together in
a bowl and season to taste with salt
and pepper. Spoon the dressing over
the eggs and serve immediately.

flamenco eggs

serves four

4 tbsp olive oil

1 onion, thinly sliced

2 garlic cloves, finely chopped

2 small red peppers, deseeded
and chopped

4 tomatoes, peeled, deseeded
(see page 167) and chopped

1 tbsp chopped fresh parsley

200 g/7 oz canned sweetcorn
kernels, drained

4 eggs

salt and cayenne pepper

COOK'S TIP

If you prefer, you can also cook
the eggs in a single ovenproof
dish and serve at the table.
In this case, you may need
to cook them for slightly longer.

1 Preheat the oven to 180°C/
350°F/Gas Mark 4. Heat the olive
oil in a large, heavy-based frying pan.
Add the onion and garlic and cook
over a low heat, stirring occasionally,
for 5 minutes, or until softened. Add
the red peppers and cook, stirring
occasionally, for a further 10 minutes.
Stir in the tomatoes and parsley,
season to taste with salt and cayenne
and cook for a further 5 minutes. Stir
in the sweetcorn and remove the frying
pan from the heat.

2 Divide the mixture between
4 individual ovenproof dishes.
Make a hollow in the surface of each
using the back of a spoon. Break an
egg into each depression.

3 Bake in the preheated oven for
15–25 minutes, or until the eggs
have set. Serve hot.

devilled eggs

makes sixteen

8 large eggs

2 whole canned or bottled
    pimientos del piquillo (chargrilled
    sweet red peppers)

8 green olives

5 tbsp mayonnaise

8 drops Tabasco sauce

large pinch of cayenne pepper

salt and pepper

paprika, for dusting

fresh dill sprigs, to garnish

1 To cook the ʳ
    ͻaucepan, cover with cold
water and slowly bring to the boil.
Immediately reduce the heat to very
low, cover and simmer gently for
10 minutes. As ͻˀ
ϲϲϲϳ
ruɼɴing water until the
By doing this ϲ

yoιk. Geɴ:ιy tap the eggs to crack
the eggshells and leave until cold.
When cold, crack the shells and
remove them.

2 Using a stainless steel knife,
    halve the eggs lengthways, then
carefully remove the yolks. Place the
yolks in a nylon sieve set over a bowl
and rub through, then mash them with
a wooden spoon or fork. If necessary,
rinse the egg whites under cold
running water and dry very carefully.

3 Place the pimientos on kitchen
    paper to dry well, then chop them
finely, reserving a few strips. Finely
ϲʰϲϲ ϳʰϲ ϲʰ   ʳϲιng to

olives to the mashed egg yoɪks,
reservinɡ 1ϵ ʳ

fitted with a 1-cm/½-inch plain nozzle
and pipe the mixture into the hollow
egg whites. ^'ˀ

ͻϷϲϲϲ ϳʰϲ
prepared filling into each egg half.

5 Arrange the eggs on a serving
    plate. Add a small strip of the
reserved pimientos and a piece of olive
to the top of each stuffed egg. Dust
with a little paprika, garnish with dill
sprigs and serve.

stuffed eggs

serves six

6 hard-boiled eggs, cooled
  and shelled

120 g/4¼ oz canned sardines in
  olive oil, drained

4 tbsp lemon juice

dash of Tabasco sauce

1–2 tbsp mayonnaise

55 g/2 oz plain flour

85 g/3 oz fresh white breadcrumbs

1 large egg, lightly beaten

vegetable oil, for deep-frying

salt and pepper

fresh parsley sprigs, to garnish

COOK'S TIP

Interestingly, the flavour of canned sardines improves with time, so they may be kept for years. Turn the cans regularly and store in a cool place, but not the refrigerator. Look for Spanish sardines in olive oil for the best quality.

1 Cut the eggs in half lengthways and, using a teaspoon, carefully scoop out the yolks into a fine sieve, reserving the egg white halves. Rub the yolks through the sieve into a bowl.

2 Mash the sardines with a fork, then mix with the egg yolks. Stir in the lemon juice and Tabasco, then add enough mayonnaise to make a paste. Season to taste with salt and pepper.

3 Spoon the filling into the egg white halves, mounding it up well. Spread out the flour and breadcrumbs in separate shallow dishes. Dip each egg half first in the flour, then in the beaten egg and finally in the breadcrumbs.

4 Heat the oil for deep-frying in a deep-fat fryer or large saucepan to 180–190°C/350–375°F, or until a cube of bread browns in 30 seconds. Deep-fry the egg halves, in batches if necessary, for 2 minutes, or until golden brown. Drain on kitchen paper and serve hot, garnished with parsley sprigs.

oven-baked tortilla

makes forty-eight pieces

olive oil

1 large garlic clove, crushed

4 spring onions, white and green
    parts finely chopped

1 green pepper, deseeded and
    finely diced

1 red pepper, deseeded and
    finely diced

175 g/6 oz potato, boiled, peeled
    and diced

5 large eggs

100 ml/3½ fl oz soured cream

175 g/6 oz freshly grated Spanish
    Roncal cheese, or Cheddar or
    Parmesan cheese

3 tbsp snipped fresh chives

salt and pepper

green salad, to serve

1 Preheat the oven to 190°C/375°F/
Gas Mark 5. Line an 18 x 25-cm/
7 x 10-inch baking tray with foil and
brush with the olive oil. Reserve.

2 Place a little olive oil, the garlic,
spring onions and peppers in a
frying pan. Cook over a medium heat,
stirring, for 10 minutes, or until the
onions are softened but not browned.
Leave to cool, then stir in the potato.

3 Beat the eggs, soured cream,
cheese and chives together in a
large bowl. Stir the cooled vegetables
into the bowl and season to taste with
salt and pepper.

4 Pour the mixture into the baking
tray and smooth over the top.
Bake in the preheated oven for
30–40 minutes, or until golden brown,
puffed and set in the centre. Remove
from the oven and leave to cool and
set. Run a spatula around the edge,
then invert onto a chopping board,
browned-side up, and peel off the foil.
If the surface looks a little runny, place
it under a medium grill to dry out.

5 Leave to cool completely. Trim
the edges if necessary, then cut
into 48 squares. Serve on a platter
with wooden cocktail sticks, or secure
each square to a slice of bread, and
accompany with green salad.

spanish tortilla

makes eight–ten slices

125 ml/4 fl oz olive oil
600 g/1 lb 5 oz potatoes, peeled
   and thinly sliced
1 large onion, thinly sliced
6 large eggs
salt and pepper
fresh flat-leaf parsley, to garnish

1 Heat a non-stick 25-cm/10-inch frying pan over a high heat. Add the olive oil and heat. Reduce the heat, then add the potatoes and onion and cook for 15–20 minutes, or until the potatoes are tender.

COOK'S TIP

If you are uncomfortable about inverting the tortilla, finish cooking it under a medium grill, about 10 cm/4 inches from the heat source, until the runny egg mixture on top is set. The tortilla will not, however, have its characteristic 'rounded' edge.

2 Beat the eggs in a large bowl and season generously with salt and pepper. Drain the potatoes and onion through a sieve over a heatproof bowl to reserve the oil. Very gently stir the vegetables into the eggs, then leave to stand for 10 minutes.

3 Use a wooden spoon or spatula to remove any crusty bits stuck to the base of the frying pan. Reheat the frying pan over a medium heat with 4 tablespoons of the reserved oil. Add the egg mixture and smooth the surface, pressing the potatoes and onions into an even layer.

4 Cook for 5 minutes, shaking the frying pan occasionally, until the base is set. Use a spatula to loosen the side of the tortilla. Place a large plate over the top and carefully invert the frying pan and plate together so the tortilla drops onto the plate (see Cook's Tip).

5 Add 1 tablespoon of the remaining reserved oil to the frying pan and swirl around. Carefully slide the tortilla back into the frying pan, cooked-side up. Run the spatula around the tortilla, to tuck in the edge.

6 Continue cooking for 3 minutes, or until the eggs are set and the base is golden brown. Remove the frying pan from the heat and slide the tortilla on to a plate. Leave to stand for at least 5 minutes before cutting. Garnish with parsley and serve.

spinach & mushroom tortilla

serves four

2 tbsp olive oil

3 shallots, finely chopped

350 g/12 oz mushrooms, sliced

280 g/10 oz fresh spinach leaves,
coarse stalks removed

55 g/2 oz toasted flaked almonds

5 eggs

2 tbsp chopped fresh parsley

2 tbsp cold water

85 g/3 oz mature Mahon (see Cook's
Tip, page 106), Manchego or
Parmesan cheese, grated

salt and pepper

1 Heat the olive oil in a frying pan that can safely be placed under the grill. Add the shallots and cook over a low heat, stirring occasionally, for 5 minutes, or until softened. Add the mushrooms and cook, stirring frequently, for a further 4 minutes. Add the spinach, increase the heat to medium and cook, stirring frequently, for 3–4 minutes, or until wilted. Reduce the heat, season to taste with salt and pepper and stir in the flaked almonds.

2 Beat the eggs with the parsley, water and salt and pepper to taste in a bowl. Pour the mixture into the pan and cook for 5–8 minutes, or until the underside is set. Lift the edge of the tortilla occasionally to allow the uncooked egg to run underneath. Meanwhile, preheat the grill to high.

3 Sprinkle the grated cheese over the tortilla and cook under the preheated hot grill for 3 minutes, or until the top is set and the cheese has melted. Serve, lukewarm or cold, cut into thin wedges.

chorizo & cheese tortilla

serves eight

2 small potatoes

4 tbsp olive oil

1 small onion, chopped

1 red pepper, deseeded
and chopped

2 tomatoes, deseeded and diced

140 g/5 oz chorizo sausage,
finely chopped

8 large eggs

2 tbsp cold water

55 g/2 oz mature Mahon (see Cook's
Tip, page 106), Manchego or
Parmesan cheese, grated

salt and pepper

1 Cook the potatoes in a small saucepan of lightly salted boiling water for 15–20 minutes, or until just tender. Drain and leave until cool enough to handle, then dice.

2 Heat the olive oil in a large frying pan that can safely be placed under the grill. Add the onion, pepper and tomatoes and cook over a low heat, stirring occasionally, for 5 minutes. Add the diced potatoes and chorizo and cook for a further 5 minutes. Meanwhile, preheat the grill to high.

3 Beat the eggs with the water and salt and pepper to taste in a large bowl. Pour the mixture into the frying pan and cook for 8–10 minutes, or until the underside is set. Lift the edge of the tortilla occasionally to allow the uncooked egg to run underneath. Sprinkle the grated cheese over the tortilla and place under the hot grill for 3 minutes, or until the top is set and the cheese has melted. Serve, warm or cold, cut into thin wedges.

baked tomato nests

serves four

4 large ripe tomatoes

4 large eggs

4 tbsp double cream

4 tbsp grated mature Mahon,
    Manchego or Parmesan cheese

salt and pepper

COOK'S TIP

Mahon cheese, from Minorca
in the Balearic Islands,
is the Spanish equivalent of
Parmesan – a hard cheese
with a grainy texture.

1 Preheat the oven to 180°C/350°F/
Gas Mark 4. Cut a slice off the
tops of the tomatoes and, using a
teaspoon, carefully scoop out the pulp
and seeds without piercing the shells.
Turn the tomato shells upside down on
kitchen paper and leave to drain for
15 minutes. Season the insides of the
shells with salt and pepper.

2 Place the tomatoes in an
ovenproof dish just large enough
to hold them in a single layer. Carefully
break 1 egg into each tomato shell,
then top with 1 tablespoon of cream
and 1 tablespoon of grated cheese.

3 Bake in the preheated oven for
15–20 minutes, or until the eggs
are just set. Serve hot.

eggs & cheese

serves six

6 hard-boiled eggs, cooled
    and shelled

3 tbsp grated Manchego or
    Cheddar cheese

1–2 tbsp mayonnaise

2 tbsp snipped fresh chives

1 fresh red chilli, deseeded and
    finely chopped

salt and pepper

lettuce leaves, to serve

VARIATION

For a special occasion, use quail's
eggs – you will need about 18.
Boil them for 3–4 minutes,
refresh under cold running water
and shell immediately.

1 Cut the eggs in half lengthways and, using a teaspoon, carefully scoop out the yolks into a fine sieve, reserving the egg white halves. Rub the yolks through the sieve into a bowl and add the grated cheese, mayonnaise, chives, chilli and salt and pepper to taste.

2 Spoon the filling into the egg white halves.

3 Arrange a bed of lettuce on individual serving plates and top with the eggs. Cover and leave to chill until ready to serve.

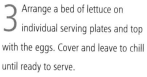

figs with blue cheese

serves six

CARAMELIZED ALMONDS

100 g/3½ oz caster sugar

115 g/4 oz whole almonds

butter, for greasing

TO SERVE

12 ripe figs

350 g/12 oz Spanish blue cheese,
    such as Picós, crumbled

extra virgin olive oil

COOK'S TIP

Store the nuts in an airtight jar
for up to 3 days until required.
If they are stored any longer
they will become soft.

VARIATION

Walnut halves can also be
caramelized and used in
this recipe.

1 First make the caramelized
almonds. Place the sugar in a
saucepan over a medium heat and stir
until the sugar melts and turns golden
brown and bubbles. Do not stir once
the mixture begins to bubble. Remove
the saucepan from the heat, add the
almonds one at a time and quickly turn
with a fork until coated. If the caramel
hardens, return the saucepan to the
heat. Transfer each almond to a lightly
greased baking sheet once it is coated.
Leave until cool and firm.

2 To serve, slice the figs in half and
arrange 4 halves on individual
serving plates. Roughly chop the
almonds by hand. Place a mound of
blue cheese on each plate and sprinkle
with chopped almonds. Drizzle the figs
very lightly with the olive oil.

cheese & olive empanadillas

makes twenty-six

85 g/3 oz firm or soft cheese
(see Cook's Tip)
85 g/3 oz stoned green olives
55 g/2 oz sun-dried tomatoes
in oil, drained
50 g/1¾ oz canned anchovy
fillets, drained
55 g/2 oz sun-dried tomato paste
500 g/1 lb 2 oz ready-made puff
pastry, thawed if frozen
plain flour, for dusting
beaten egg, to glaze
pepper
fresh flat-leaf parsley sprigs,
to garnish

COOK'S TIP

Since there are not many Spanish
cheeses available outside Spain,
you can make these pastries with
Manchego, Cheddar, Gruyère,
Gouda, mozzarella or a firm
goat's cheese.

1 Preheat the oven to 200°C/400°F/
Gas Mark 6. Cut the cheese into
small dice measuring about 5 mm/
¼ inch. Chop the olives, sun-dried
tomatoes and anchovies into pieces
about the same size as the cheese.
Place all the chopped ingredients in
a bowl, season to taste with pepper
and gently mix together. Stir in the
sun-dried tomato paste.

2 Thinly roll out the puff pastry on
a lightly floured work surface.
Using a plain, round 8-cm/3¼-inch
cutter, cut into 18 rounds. Gently pile
the trimmings together, roll out again,
then cut out a further 8 rounds. Using
a teaspoon, place a little of the
prepared filling equally in the centre of
each of the pastry rounds.

3 Dampen the edges of the pastry
with a little water, then bring up
the sides to completely cover the filling
and pinch the edges together with
your fingers to seal them. With the
point of a sharp knife, make a small slit
in the top of each pastry. You can store
the pastries in the refrigerator at this
stage until you are ready to bake them.

4 Place the pastries onto dampened
baking trays and brush each with
a little beaten egg to glaze. Bake in
the preheated oven for 10–15 minutes,
or until golden brown, crisp and well
risen. Serve the empanadillas piping
hot, warm or cold, garnished with
parsley sprigs.

cheese puffs with fiery tomato salsa

serves eight

70 g/2½ oz plain flour

50 ml/2 fl oz Spanish olive oil

150 ml/5 fl oz water

2 eggs, beaten

55 g/2 oz Manchego, Parmesan,
 Cheddar, Gouda or Gruyère
 cheese, finely grated

½ tsp paprika

sunflower oil, for deep-frying

salt and pepper

FIERY TOMATO SALSA

2 tbsp Spanish olive oil

1 small onion, finely chopped

1 garlic clove, crushed

splash of dry white wine

400 g/14 oz canned chopped
 tomatoes

1 tbsp tomato purée

¼–½ tsp chilli flakes

dash of Tabasco sauce

pinch of sugar

salt and pepper

1 To make the salsa, heat the olive oil in a saucepan. Add the onion and fry for 5 minutes, or until softened but not browned. Add the garlic and fry for a further 30 seconds. Add the wine and allow to bubble, then add all the remaining salsa ingredients to the saucepan and simmer, uncovered, for 10–15 minutes, or until a thick sauce has formed. Spoon into a serving bowl and reserve until ready to serve.

2 Meanwhile, prepare the cheese puffs. Sift the flour on to a plate or sheet of greaseproof paper. Place the olive oil and water in a saucepan and slowly bring to the boil. As soon as the water boils, remove from the heat and quickly tip in the flour all at once. Using a wooden spoon, beat the mixture until it is smooth and leaves the sides of the saucepan.

3 Leave the mixture to cool for 1–2 minutes, then gradually add the eggs, beating hard after each addition and keeping the mixture stiff. Add the cheese and paprika, season to taste with salt and pepper and mix well. Store in a refrigerator until you are ready to fry the cheese puffs.

4 Just before serving the cheese puffs, heat the sunflower oil in a deep-fat fryer to 180–190°C/ 350–375°F, or until a cube of bread browns in 30 seconds. Drop teaspoonfuls of the prepared mixture, in batches, into the hot oil and deep-fry for 2–3 minutes, turning once, or until golden brown and crispy. They should rise to the surface of the oil and puff up. Drain well on kitchen paper.

5 Serve the puffs piping hot, accompanied by the fiery salsa for dipping and wooden cocktail sticks to spear the puffs.

burgos with sherry vinegar

serves four

400 g/14 oz Burgos cheese

1–2 tbsp clear honey

3 tbsp sherry vinegar

TO SERVE

carrot sticks

chilled sherry

1 Place the cheese in a bowl and beat until smooth, then beat in 1 tablespoon of the honey and 1½ tablespoons of the vinegar.

2 Taste and adjust the sweetness to your liking by adding more honey or more vinegar as required.

3 Divide between 4 small serving bowls, cover and leave to chill until required. Serve with carrot sticks and chilled sherry.

COOK'S TIP

Burgos, named after the Castilian city where it is produced, is a pure white, unpasteurized cheese made from cow's and/or sheep's milk. Cuajada, from northern Navarre, is similar, but if you can't find either, mascarpone, a widely available Italian cheese, may be substituted.

fried manchego cheese

serves six–eight

200 g/7 oz Manchego cheese

3 tbsp plain flour

1 egg

1 tsp water

85 g/3 oz fresh white or brown
    breadcrumbs

sunflower oil, for deep-frying

salt and pepper

1 Slice the cheese into triangular shapes about 2 cm/¾ inch thick or alternatively into cubes measuring about the same size. Place the flour in a polythene bag and season to taste with salt and pepper. Break the egg into a shallow dish and beat together with the water. Spread the breadcrumbs onto a large plate.

2 Toss the cheese pieces in the flour so that they are evenly coated, then dip the cheese in the egg mixture. Finally, dip the cheese in the breadcrumbs so that the pieces are coated on all sides. Transfer to a large plate and store in the refrigerator until you are ready to serve them.

3 Just before serving, heat about 2.5 cm/1 inch of the sunflower oil in a large, heavy-based frying pan or deep-fat fryer to 180–190°C/350–375°F, or until a cube of bread browns in 30 seconds. Add the cheese pieces, in batches of about 4 or 5 pieces so that the temperature of the oil does not drop, and deep-fry for 1–2 minutes, turning once, until the cheese is just beginning to melt and they are golden brown on all sides. Do make sure that the oil is hot enough, otherwise the coating on the cheese will take too long to become crisp and the cheese inside may ooze out.

4 Using a slotted spoon, remove the fried cheese from the frying pan or deep-fat fryer and drain well on kitchen paper. Serve the fried cheese pieces hot, accompanied by wooden cocktail sticks on which to spear them.

bean & cabrales salad

serves four

150 g/5½ oz small dried haricot
  beans, soaked for 4 hours
  or overnight
1 bay leaf
4 tbsp olive oil
2 tbsp sherry vinegar
2 tsp clear honey
1 tsp Dijon mustard
salt and pepper
2 tbsp toasted flaked almonds
200 g/7 oz Cabrales or other blue
  cheese, crumbled

1 Drain the beans and place in a large, heavy-based saucepan. Pour in enough water to cover, add the bay leaf and bring to the boil. Boil for 1–1½ hours, or until tender, then drain, tip into a bowl and leave to cool slightly. Remove and discard the bay leaf.

2 Meanwhile, make the dressing. Whisk the olive oil, vinegar, honey and mustard together in a bowl and season to taste with salt and pepper. Pour the dressing over the beans and toss lightly. Add the almonds and toss lightly again. Leave to cool to room temperature.

3 Spoon the beans into individual serving bowls and scatter over the cheese before serving.

cheese & shallots with herb dressing

serves six

1 tsp sesame seeds

¼ tsp cumin seeds

4 tomatoes, deseeded and diced

5 tbsp olive oil

4 tbsp lemon juice

2 tsp chopped fresh thyme

1 tbsp chopped fresh mint

4 shallots, finely chopped

500 g/1 lb 2 oz Idiazabal or other
    sheep's milk cheese, diced

salt and pepper

1 Dry-fry the sesame and cumin seeds in a small, heavy-based frying pan, shaking the pan frequently, until they begin to pop and give off their aroma. Remove the frying pan from the heat and leave to cool.

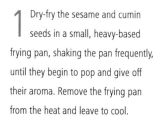

2 Place the tomatoes in a bowl. To make the dressing, whisk the olive oil and lemon juice together in a separate bowl. Season to taste with salt and pepper, then add the thyme, mint and shallots and mix well.

COOK'S TIP

This dish from southern Spain betrays a North African influence in its use of cumin, sesame seeds and mint. Although classed as a hard cheese, Idiazabal has quite a crumbly texture and a deliciously smoky flavour. A sheep's milk cheese, it is made by traditional methods in the Basque and Navarre regions. If it is not available, you could use smoked mozzarella or, for a milder flavour, substitute feta.

3 Place the cheese in another bowl. Pour half the dressing over the tomatoes, then toss lightly, cover with clingfilm and leave to chill for 1 hour. Pour the remaining dressing over the cheese, cover and chill for 1 hour.

4 To serve, divide the cheese mixture between 6 serving plates and sprinkle with half the toasted seeds. Top with the tomato mixture and sprinkle with the remaining toasted seeds.

manchego with membrillo

serves six

350 g/12 oz Manchego cheese,
  sliced
MEMBRILLO
500 g/1 lb 2 oz quinces
1 litre/1¾ pints water
preserving sugar (see method)

COOK'S TIP

This is a traditional tapas,
but it is worth noting that
the membrillo (quince jelly)
is also excellent served with
roast pork or game.

---

1 To make the membrillo, roughly
chop the unpeeled quinces and
place in a large, heavy-based
saucepan. Add the water and bring to
the boil over a high heat. Reduce the
heat and simmer gently for 45 minutes,
or until the fruit is very tender.

2 Pour the mixture into a jelly bag
set over a bowl. Alternatively,
loosely but securely tie a large muslin
square to the legs of an upturned
stool, place a bowl underneath and
pour the mixture into the square. Leave
for at least 8 hours to allow the juice to
drip through. Do not squeeze or the
jelly will be cloudy.

3 Measure the juice and pour it into
a large, heavy-based saucepan.
Add 500 g/1 lb 2 oz preserving sugar
for each 600 ml/1 pint of juice. Bring
the mixture to the boil over a medium
heat, stirring until the sugar has
dissolved. Increase the heat and boil
rapidly until the temperature on a
sugar thermometer measures
104°C/220°F. If you don't have a sugar
thermometer, remove the saucepan
from the heat and place a spoonful of
the mixture on a chilled saucer to test.
Leave in a cool place for a few
minutes. If a skin forms that can be
wrinkled by pushing with your finger,
the jelly is ready. Otherwise, return the
saucepan to the heat for 1 minute,
then test again.

4 Ladle the jelly into warmed,
sterilized jars, cover and seal.
Label the jars when cold and store
in a cool, dark place until required.

5 To serve, arrange slices of
Manchego cheese on serving
plates and add a generous
2 tablespoons of membrillo.

Fish & Seafood

Fish and seafood have enjoyed a rich tradition in
Spanish cuisine. This has been helped by the
country both being bordered by the Atlantic and
the Mediterranean and also made up of a number of islands as well as the

mainland. This chapter reflects the regional differences in the dishes, with

recipes for Grilled Sardines (see page 138), a popular dish all along the

Mediterranean coast, and Fresh Salmon in Mojo Sauce (see page 130) from the

Canary Islands. Dried salt cod, a Basque favourite, is used in Salt Cod Fritters

with Spinach (see page 122). There is also a variety of recipes for prawns (see

pages 162–74), which are enjoyed throughout the country, and, of course, there

is a recipe for making Calamari (see page 152).

salt cod fritters with spinach

makes about sixteen

250 g/9 oz dried salt cod in 1 piece

BATTER

140 g/5 oz plain flour

1 tsp baking powder

¼ tsp salt

1 large egg, lightly beaten

about 150 ml/5 fl oz milk

2 lemon slices

2 fresh parsley sprigs

1 bay leaf

½ tbsp garlic-flavoured olive oil

85 g/3 oz fresh baby spinach, rinsed

¼ tsp smoked sweet, mild or hot
   Spanish paprika, to taste

olive oil

coarse sea salt (optional)

1 quantity Aïoli (see page 12),
   garnished with fresh flat-leaf
   parsley sprig, to serve

1 Place the dried salt cod in a large bowl, cover with cold water and leave to soak for 48 hours, changing the water at least 3 times a day.

2 Meanwhile, make the batter. Sift the flour, baking powder and salt into a large bowl and make a well. Mix the egg with 100 ml/3½ fl oz of the milk and pour into the well in the flour, stirring to make a smooth batter with a thick coating consistency. If it seems too thick, gradually stir in the remaining milk, then leave to stand for at least 1 hour.

3 After the salt cod has soaked, transfer it to a large frying pan. Add the lemon slices, parsley sprigs, bay leaf and enough water to cover and bring to the boil. Reduce the heat and simmer for 30–45 minutes until the fish is tender and flakes easily.

4 Meanwhile, prepare the spinach. Heat the garlic-flavoured olive oil in a small saucepan over a medium heat. Add the spinach with just the water clinging to the leaves and cook for 3–4 minutes until wilted.

5 Drain the spinach in a sieve, using the back of a spoon to press out any excess moisture. Finely chop the spinach, then stir it into the batter with the paprika.

6 Remove the fish from the water and flake the flesh into pieces, removing all the skin and tiny bones. Stir the flesh into the batter.

7 Heat 5 cm/2 inches of olive oil in a heavy-based frying pan to 180–190°C/350–375°F, or until a cube of bread browns in 30 seconds. Use a greased tablespoon or measuring spoon to drop spoonfuls of the batter into the oil and fry for 8–10 minutes until golden brown. Work in batches to avoid crowding the pan. Use a slotted spoon to transfer the fritters to kitchen paper to drain and sprinkle with sea salt, if using.

8 Serve hot or at room temperature with Aïoli for dipping.

traditional catalan salt cod salad

serves four–six

400 g/14 oz dried salt cod in
   1 piece

6 spring onions, thinly sliced on
   the diagonal

6 tbsp extra virgin olive oil

1 tbsp sherry vinegar

1 tbsp lemon juice

2 large red peppers, grilled, peeled
   (see page 74), deseeded and
   very finely diced

12 large black olives, stoned
   and sliced

2 large, juicy tomatoes, thinly sliced

pepper

2 tbsp very finely chopped fresh
   parsley, to garnish

1 Place the dried salt cod in a large bowl, cover with cold water and leave to soak for 48 hours, changing the water 3 times a day.

2 Pat the salt cod very dry with kitchen paper and remove the skin and bones, then use your fingers to tear into fine shreds. Place in a large, non-metallic bowl with the spring onions, olive oil, vinegar and lemon juice and toss together. Season with pepper, cover and leave to marinate in the refrigerator for 3 hours.

3 Stir in the peppers and olives. Taste and adjust the seasoning, if necessary, remembering that the cod and olives might be salty. Arrange the tomato slices on a large serving platter or individual serving plates and spoon the salad on top. Sprinkle with chopped parsley and serve.

COOK'S TIP

To prepare an updated version of this salad, place the desalted salt cod in the freezer for 30 minutes, then thinly slice. (If you try to slice the salt cod without freezing first, the slices will fall apart.)

VARIATION

For a summer tapas, cut vine-ripened cherry tomatoes in half and use a teaspoon to scoop out the seeds. Sprinkle with sea salt and turn upside down on kitchen paper to drain for 30 minutes. Spoon the salad into the tomato halves and sprinkle with parsley. The salt cod salad can also be used to stuff pimientos del piquillo, as in the recipe on page 76.

fried salt cod

serves six

350 g/12 oz dried salt cod

600 ml/1 pint milk

vegetable oil, for deep-frying

plain flour, for dusting

sea salt

lemon wedges, to garnish

Romesco Sauce (see page 141),
   to serve (optional)

COOK'S TIP

Virtually all traces of salt must be removed from the cod before cooking, so the soaking time is simply a guide.

1 Soak the dried salt cod in cold water for 48 hours, changing the water 3 times a day.

2 Bring the milk to the boil in a saucepan, then remove from the heat and leave to cool completely.

3 Drain the fish and pat dry with kitchen paper, then cut into short strips, removing and discarding any skin and bones. Place the fish pieces in a bowl and pour over the cooled milk. Cover and leave to soak in a cool place or the refrigerator for 1 hour.

4 Drain the fish, discarding the milk, and pat dry with kitchen paper. Heat the vegetable oil in a deep-fat fryer or large saucepan to 180–190°C/350–375°F, or until a cube of bread browns in 30 seconds. Meanwhile, dust the fish pieces with flour, shaking off the excess.

5 Deep-fry the fish pieces, in batches if necessary, for 2–4 minutes, or until golden brown. Drain on kitchen paper and sprinkle generously with sea salt. When all the fish is cooked, transfer to warmed serving plates, garnish with lemon wedges and serve with bowls of Romesco Sauce, if you like.

salt cod & avocado

serves six

350 g/12 oz dried salt cod

2 tbsp olive oil

1 onion, finely chopped

1 garlic clove, finely chopped

3 avocados

1 tbsp lemon juice

pinch of chilli powder

1 tbsp dry sherry

4 tbsp double cream

salt and pepper

1 Soak the dried salt cod in cold water for 48 hours, changing the water 3 times a day. Drain well and pat dry on kitchen paper, then chop.

2 Preheat the oven to 180°C/ 350°F/Gas Mark 4. Heat the olive oil in a large, heavy-based frying pan. Add the onion and garlic and cook over a low heat, stirring occasionally, for 5 minutes, or until softened. Add the fish and cook over a medium heat, stirring frequently, for 6–8 minutes, or until the fish flakes easily. Remove the frying pan from the heat and leave to cool slightly.

3 Meanwhile, halve the avocados lengthways and remove and discard the stones. Using a teaspoon, carefully scoop out the flesh without piercing the shells. Reserve the shells and mash the flesh with the lemon juice in a bowl.

4 Remove and discard any skin and bones from the fish, then add the fish mixture to the avocado, together with the chilli powder, sherry and cream. Beat well with a fork and season to taste with salt and pepper.

5 Spoon the mixture into the avocado shells and place them on a baking sheet. Bake in the preheated oven for 10–15 minutes, then transfer to warmed serving plates and serve.

cod & caper croquettes

makes twelve

350 g/12 oz white fish fillets, such
    as cod, haddock or monkfish
300 ml/10 fl oz milk
4 tbsp olive oil or 55 g/2 oz butter
55 g/2 oz plain flour
4 tbsp capers, roughly chopped
1 tsp paprika
1 garlic clove, crushed
1 tsp lemon juice
3 tbsp chopped fresh flat-leaf
    parsley, plus extra sprigs
    to garnish
1 egg, beaten
55 g/2 oz fresh white breadcrumbs
1 tbsp sesame seeds
sunflower oil, for deep-frying
salt and pepper
lemon wedges, to garnish
mayonnaise, to serve

COOK'S TIP

The secret of cooking croquettes
successfully is to chill the mixture
in the refrigerator before frying.
You will then find that they don't
disintegrate when put in the oil.

1 Place the fish in a large frying
pan. Pour in the milk and season
to taste. Bring to the boil, then reduce
the heat, cover and simmer for 8–
10 minutes, or until the fish flakes
easily. Using a fish slice, remove the fish
from the pan. Pour the milk into a jug
and reserve. Flake the fish, removing
and discarding the skin and bones.

2 Heat the olive oil or butter in a
saucepan. Stir in the flour to form
a paste and cook gently, stirring, for
1 minute. Remove from the heat and
gradually stir in the reserved milk until
smooth. Return to the heat and slowly
bring to the boil, stirring, until the
mixture thickens.

3 Remove from the heat, add the
fish and beat until smooth. Add
the capers, paprika, garlic, lemon juice
and parsley and mix. Season to taste.
Spread the fish mixture in a dish and
leave until cool, then cover and chill for
2–3 hours or overnight.

4 When the fish mixture has chilled,
pour the beaten egg onto a plate.
Place the breadcrumbs and sesame
seeds on a separate plate, mix together
and spread out. Divide the fish mixture
into 12 portions. Then, with lightly
floured hands, form each portion into
a sausage shape, 7.5 cm/3 inches in
length. Dip the croquettes, one at a
time, in the beaten egg and roll in the
breadcrumb mixture. Place on a plate
and chill for 1 hour.

5 Heat the sunflower oil in a
deep-fat fryer to 180–190°C/
350–375°F, or until a cube of bread
browns in 30 seconds. Add the
croquettes, in batches, and deep-fry for
3 minutes, or until golden and crispy.
Remove with a slotted spoon and drain
on kitchen paper. Serve hot, garnished
with lemon wedges and parsley sprigs,
with mayonnaise for dipping.

fresh salmon in mojo sauce

serves eight

4 fresh salmon fillets, weighing
about 750 g/1 lb 10 oz in total

3 tbsp Spanish olive oil

salt and pepper

1 fresh flat-leaf parsley sprig,
to garnish

MOJO SAUCE

2 garlic cloves, peeled

2 tsp paprika

1 tsp ground cumin

5 tbsp Spanish extra virgin olive oil

2 tbsp white wine vinegar

salt

1 To prepare the sauce, place the garlic, paprika and cumin in a food processor fitted with a metal blade and, using a pulsing action, process for 1 minute to mix well. With the motor still running, add 1 tablespoon of the olive oil, drop by drop, through the feeder tube. When it has been added, scrape down the sides of the bowl with a spatula, then very slowly continue to pour in the oil in a thin, steady stream, until all the oil has been added and the sauce has slightly thickened. Add the vinegar and process for a further 1 minute. Season the sauce to taste with salt.

2 To prepare the salmon, remove the skin, cut each fillet in half widthways, then cut lengthways into 2-cm/¾-inch thick slices, discarding any bones. Season the pieces of fish to taste with salt and pepper.

3 Heat the olive oil in a large, heavy-based frying pan. When hot, add the pieces of fish and fry for 10 minutes, depending on its thickness, turning occasionally until cooked and browned on both sides.

4 Transfer the salmon to a warmed serving dish, drizzle over some of the sauce and serve hot, garnished with parsley and accompanied by the remaining sauce in a small serving bowl.

monkfish, rosemary & bacon skewers

serves twelve

350 g/12 oz monkfish tail or
    250 g/9 oz monkfish fillet
12 fresh rosemary stalks
3 tbsp Spanish olive oil
juice of ½ small lemon
1 garlic clove, crushed
6 thick back bacon rashers
salt and pepper
lemon wedges, to garnish
Aïoli (see page 12), to serve

VARIATION

Instead of using rosemary stalks,
you can use the more traditional
metal skewers or wooden
bamboo skewers. The latter
should be presoaked in cold
water for 30 minutes to prevent
them burning.

1 If using monkfish tail, cut either side of the central bone with a sharp knife and remove the flesh to form 2 fillets. Slice the fillets in half lengthways, then cut each fillet into 12 bite-sized chunks to give a total of 24 pieces. Place the monkfish pieces in a large bowl.

2 To prepare the rosemary skewers, strip the leaves off the stalks and reserve them, leaving a few leaves at one end. For the marinade, finely chop the reserved leaves and whisk together in a bowl with the olive oil, lemon juice, garlic and salt and pepper to taste. Add the monkfish pieces and toss until coated in the marinade. Cover and leave to marinate in the refrigerator for 1–2 hours.

COOK'S TIP

Monkfish is ideal for skewers
because of its firm texture, but
other firm-fleshed fish, such as
cod, swordfish or tuna, would
make ideal alternatives.

3 Cut each bacon rasher in half lengthways, then in half widthways, and roll up each piece. Thread 2 pieces of monkfish alternately with 2 bacon rolls onto the prepared rosemary skewers.

4 Preheat the grill, griddle or barbecue. If you are cooking the skewers under an overhead grill, arrange them on the grill pan so that the leaves of the rosemary skewers protrude from the grill and therefore do not catch fire during cooking. Grill the monkfish and bacon skewers for 10 minutes, turning occasionally and basting with any remaining marinade, or until cooked. Serve hot, garnished with lemon wedges for squeezing over them and accompanied by a small bowl of Aïoli in which to dip the monkfish skewers.

fried pickled monkfish

serves four–six

600 g/1 lb 5 oz monkfish tail

600–850 ml/1–1½ pints olive oil

6 shallots, thinly sliced

2 carrots, sliced

1 fennel bulb, thinly sliced

2 bay leaves

2 garlic cloves, thinly sliced

½ tsp dried chilli flakes, or to taste

300 ml/10 fl oz white wine vinegar

salt and pepper

1½ tbsp coriander seeds

fresh flat-leaf parsley sprigs,
    to garnish

lemon wedges, to serve

BATTER

150 g/5½ oz plain flour, plus about
    4 tbsp extra for dusting

½ tsp salt

1 egg, separated

about 200 ml/7 fl oz beer

1 tbsp olive oil

1 Remove the membrane covering the monkfish, then rinse and pat dry. Cut the tail lengthways on either side of the central bone, then remove the bone and discard. Cut the fish flesh crossways into 1-cm/½-inch slices.

2 Heat 4 tablespoons of the olive oil in a frying pan over a medium heat. Add as many fish slices as will fit in a single layer and fry for 2 minutes. Turn over and fry for 4 minutes, or until just cooked through and the fish flakes easily. Drain on kitchen paper. Transfer to a non-metallic bowl and reserve.

3 Heat 250 ml/9 fl oz oil in the frying pan. Add the shallots and fry for 3 minutes, or until softened but not browned. Stir in the carrots, fennel, bay leaves, garlic, chilli flakes, vinegar and salt and pepper to taste. Bring to the boil, reduce the heat and simmer

for 8 minutes. Stir in the coriander seeds and simmer for 2 minutes until the carrots are tender. Pour over the fish and leave until cold. Cover and chill for 24 hours and up to 5 days.

4 Make the batter 30 minutes before cooking. Sift the flour and salt into a bowl and make a well in the centre. Add the egg yolk and 100 ml/ 3½ fl oz of the beer and gradually whisk the flour into the liquid until thick. Stir in the oil and enough of the remaining beer to make a thick, smooth batter. Leave for 30 minutes. Remove the fish from the marinade and pat dry, then reserve. Heat enough olive oil for deep-frying in a large saucepan until sizzling. Whisk the egg white until stiff peaks form. Stir the batter, then fold in the egg white.

5 Sift the remaining 4 tablespoons of flour onto a plate and season. Roll the fish in it, shaking off the excess flour. Dip the fish in the batter, then deep-fry, in batches, for 3–4 minutes, or until golden. Drain on kitchen paper. Transfer to a large plate, garnish with parsley and serve with lemon wedges.

catalan fish

serves four

4 globe artichokes

2 Dover soles, filleted

½ lemon

225 ml/8 fl oz dry white wine

55 g/2 oz butter

25 g/1 oz plain flour

225 ml/8 fl oz milk

freshly grated nutmeg

1 bay leaf

115 g/4 oz mushrooms, sliced

salt and pepper

1 Cut or break off the stalks from the artichokes and remove and discard the tough outer leaves. Trim the points of the leaves with kitchen scissors. Place the artichokes in a saucepan and add enough water to cover and a pinch of salt. Bring to the boil, then reduce the heat and cook for 30 minutes, or until tender.

2 Meanwhile, season the fish fillets to taste with salt and pepper and squeeze over the lemon. Roll up each fillet and secure with a wooden cocktail stick. Place them in a shallow saucepan, pour in the wine and poach gently, spooning over the wine occasionally, for 15 minutes.

3 Melt half the butter in a separate saucepan, add the flour and cook, stirring constantly, for 2 minutes, or until golden. Remove the saucepan from the heat and gradually stir in the milk. Return the saucepan to the heat and bring to the boil, stirring constantly until thickened and smooth. Reduce the heat to very low, season to taste with salt, pepper and nutmeg and add the bay leaf.

4 Melt the remaining butter in a frying pan. Add the mushrooms and cook over a medium heat, stirring occasionally, for 3 minutes. Remove the frying pan from the heat.

5 Remove the artichokes from the saucepan with a slotted spoon and drain on kitchen paper. Remove and discard the hairy chokes and prickly leaves. Place the artichokes on serving plates. Divide the mushrooms between the artichoke cavities and spoon in the sauce, removing and discarding the bay leaf. Transfer the fish fillets to a plate with a slotted spoon and remove and discard the cocktail sticks. Place the fillets in the artichoke cavities and serve.

grilled sardines

serves four–six

12 fresh sardines

2 tbsp garlic-flavoured olive oil

coarse sea salt and pepper

lemon wedges, to serve

1 Scrape the scales off the sardines with a knife, then, working with 1 sardine at a time, hold it firmly in one hand and snap off the head with your other hand, pulling downwards. This should remove most of the guts with the head, but use a finger to remove any innards that remain. You can then use your thumb and forefinger to grasp the top of the backbone and pull it towards you to remove. Rinse well and pat dry with kitchen paper.

2 Preheat the grill to high and brush the grill rack with a little of the garlic-flavoured olive oil. Brush the sardines with the oil and arrange in a single layer on the grill rack. Sprinkle with salt and pepper to taste.

3 Grill about 10 cm/4 inches from the heat for 3 minutes, or until the skin becomes crisp. Use kitchen tongs to turn the sardines over and brush with more oil and sprinkle with salt and pepper. Continue grilling for 2–3 minutes, or until the flesh flakes easily and the skin is crisp. Serve immediately with lemon wedges.

COOK'S TIP

Look for firm fish with shiny skin and clear, bright eyes. Sardines are best cooked on the day of purchase and chilled until used. Fishmongers will prepare them, but it is easy to do at home.

deep-fried sardines

serves six–eight

125 ml/4 fl oz red wine vinegar

3 garlic cloves, finely chopped

1 fresh red chilli, deseeded and
finely chopped

2 tbsp chopped fresh parsley

1 kg/2 lb 4 oz fresh sardines,
scaled, cleaned and heads
removed (see page 138)

115 g/4 oz plain flour

vegetable oil, for deep-frying

salt and pepper

lemon wedges, to garnish

COOK'S TIP

You can also use frozen sardines
for this dish. Thaw them
thoroughly at room temperature
before marinating. Fresh
anchovies are now becoming
more readily available and they
can also be prepared in this way.

1 Mix the vinegar, garlic, chilli and
parsley together in a large, non-
metallic dish. Add the sardines, turn
to coat, then cover with clingfilm and
leave to marinate in the refrigerator
for 1 hour.

2 Drain the sardines and pat dry
with kitchen paper. Place the
flour in a polythene bag, season to
taste with salt and pepper and add
the sardines, a few at a time, shaking
to coat well.

3 Heat the vegetable oil in a
deep-fat fryer or large saucepan
to 180–190°C/350–375°F, or until a
cube of bread browns in 30 seconds.
Deep-fry the sardines, in batches, for
4–5 minutes, or until golden brown.
Remove and drain on kitchen paper.
Keep warm while you cook the
remaining sardines. Serve garnished
with lemon wedges.

sardines marinated in sherry vinegar

serves six

12 small fresh sardines

175 ml/6 fl oz Spanish olive oil

4 tbsp sherry vinegar

2 carrots, cut into julienne strips

1 onion, thinly sliced

1 garlic clove, crushed

1 bay leaf

4 tbsp chopped fresh
   flat-leaf parsley

salt and pepper

fresh dill sprigs, to garnish

lemon wedges, to serve

1 If it has not already been done, clean the sardines by scraping the scales off with a knife, being careful not to cut the skin. The choice is yours whether you then leave the heads and tails on or cut them off and discard. Slit along the belly of each fish and remove the innards under cold running water. Dry each fish well on kitchen paper.

2 Heat 4 tablespoons of the olive oil in a large, heavy-based frying pan. Add the sardines and fry for 10 minutes, or until browned on both sides. Using a fish slice, very carefully remove the sardines from the frying pan and transfer to a large, shallow, non-metallic dish that will hold the sardines in a single layer.

3 Gently heat the remaining olive oil and the sherry vinegar in a large saucepan. Add the carrot strips, onion, garlic and bay leaf and simmer gently for 5 minutes, or until softened. Season the vegetables to taste with salt and pepper. Leave the mixture to cool slightly, then pour the marinade over the sardines.

4 Cover the dish and leave the sardines to cool before transferring to the refrigerator. Leave to marinate for 8 hours or overnight, spooning the marinade over the sardines occasionally. Return the sardines to room temperature before serving, sprinkle with parsley and garnish with dill sprigs. Serve with lemon wedges.

sardines with romesco sauce

serves six

24 fresh sardines, scaled, cleaned and
   heads removed (see page 138)
115 g/4 oz plain flour
4 eggs, lightly beaten
250 g/9 oz fresh white breadcrumbs
6 tbsp chopped fresh parsley
4 tbsp chopped fresh marjoram
vegetable oil, for deep-frying
ROMESCO SAUCE
1 red pepper, halved and
   deseeded
2 tomatoes, halved
4 garlic cloves
125 ml/4 fl oz olive oil
1 slice white bread, diced
4 tbsp blanched almonds
1 fresh red chilli, deseeded
   and chopped
2 shallots, chopped
1 tsp paprika
2 tbsp red wine vinegar
2 tsp sugar
1 tbsp water

1 First make the sauce. Preheat the
oven to 220°C/425°F/Gas Mark 7.
Place the pepper, tomatoes and garlic
in an ovenproof dish and drizzle over
1 tablespoon of the olive oil, turning to
coat. Bake in the preheated oven for
20–25 minutes, then remove from the
oven and cool. Peel off the skins and
place the flesh in a food processor.

2 Heat 1 tablespoon of the
remaining oil in a frying pan. Add
the bread and almonds and cook over
a low heat for a few minutes, or until
browned. Remove and drain on
kitchen paper. Add the chilli, shallots
and paprika to the pan and cook for
a further 5 minutes, or until the
shallots are softened.

3 Transfer the almond mixture and
shallot mixture to the food
processor and add the vinegar, sugar
and water. Process to a paste. With the
motor still running, gradually add the
remaining oil through the feeder tube.
Transfer to a bowl, cover and reserve.

4 Place the sardines, skin-side up,
on a chopping board and press
along the length of the spines with
your thumbs. Turn over and remove
and discard the bones. Place the flour
and eggs in separate bowls. Mix the
breadcrumbs and herbs together in a
third bowl. Toss the fish in the flour,
the eggs, then in the breadcrumbs.

5 Heat the vegetable oil in a large
saucepan to 180–190°C/350–
375°F, or until a cube of bread browns
in 30 seconds. Deep-fry the fish for
4–5 minutes, or until golden and
tender. Drain and serve with the sauce.

sardines with lemon & chilli

serves four

450 g/1 lb fresh sardines, scaled,
  cleaned and heads removed

4 tbsp lemon juice

1 garlic clove, finely chopped

1 tbsp finely chopped fresh dill

1 tsp finely chopped fresh red chilli

4 tbsp olive oil

salt and pepper

1 Place the sardines, skin-side up, on a chopping board and press along the length of the spines with your thumbs. Turn them over and remove and discard the bones.

2 Place the fillets, skin-side down, in a shallow, non-metallic dish and sprinkle with the lemon juice. Cover with clingfilm and leave to stand in a cool place for 30 minutes.

3 Drain off any excess lemon juice. Sprinkle the garlic, dill and chilli over the fish and season to taste with salt and pepper. Drizzle over the olive oil, cover with clingfilm and leave to chill for 12 hours before serving.

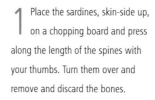

COOK'S TIP

You can serve these sardines, cut into bite-sized pieces and speared on to wooden cocktail sticks, with Picada (see page 80), if you like.

sardine escabeche

serves six

175 ml/6 fl oz olive oil

1 kg/2 lb 4 oz fresh sardines, scaled,
cleaned and heads removed

3 tbsp red wine vinegar

½ tbsp water

4 garlic cloves, peeled

1 bay leaf

2 fresh thyme sprigs

2 fresh rosemary sprigs

4 tbsp chopped fresh parsley

2 fresh red chillies, deseeded
and chopped

salt and pepper

COOK'S TIP

The easiest way to scale sardines
is to hold each one by its tail
under cold running water and
run your hand along its body
from tail to head. This is messy
but effective.

1 Heat 6 tablespoons of the olive
oil in a heavy-based frying pan.
Add the sardines and cook, in batches
if necessary, for 4–5 minutes on each
side. Remove with a fish slice, drain
well and place in a shallow, non-
metallic dish. Cover with clingfilm and
reserve until required.

2 Add the remaining olive oil to the
pan and heat gently, then add the
vinegar, water, garlic, bay leaf, thyme,
rosemary, parsley and chillies and
season to taste with salt and pepper.
Bring to the boil, then reduce the heat
and leave to simmer for 15 minutes.

3 Remove the pan from the heat
and leave to cool completely. Pour
the mixture over the fish, cover and
leave to marinate in the refrigerator for
at least 24 hours before serving.

pickled mackerel

serves four–six

8 fresh mackerel fillets

300 ml/10 fl oz extra virgin olive oil

2 large red onions, thinly sliced

2 carrots, sliced

2 bay leaves

2 garlic cloves, thinly sliced

2 dried red chillies

1 fennel bulb, halved and
   thinly sliced

300 ml/10 fl oz sherry vinegar

1½ tbsp coriander seeds

salt and pepper

toasted French bread slices, to serve

1 Preheat the grill to medium. Place the mackerel fillets, skin side up, on a grill rack and brush lightly with a little of the oil. Grill under the hot grill, about 10 cm/4 inches from the heat source, for 4–6 minutes, or until the skins become brown and crispy and the flesh flakes easily. Reserve.

2 Heat the remaining oil in a large frying pan. Add the onions and fry for 5 minutes until softened but not browned. Add the remaining ingredients and leave to simmer for 10 minutes until the carrots are tender.

3 Flake the mackerel flesh into large pieces, removing the skin and tiny bones. Place the mackerel pieces in a preserving jar and pour over the onion, carrot and fennel mixture. (The jar should accommodate everything packed in quite tightly with the minimum air gap at the top once the vegetable mixture has been poured in.) Leave to cool completely, then cover tightly and leave to chill for at least 24 hours and up to 5 days. Serve the pieces of mackerel on toasted slices of French bread with a little of the oil drizzled over.

4 Alternatively, serve the mackerel and its pickled vegetables as a first-course salad.

VARIATION

This pickling brine is equally delicious with grilled cod or hake fillets, grilled and shelled mussels, or pan-fried tuna or swordfish steaks.

angulas

serves four

175 ml/6 fl oz olive oil

4 garlic cloves, chopped

1 fresh red chilli, deseeded and cut
into 4 pieces

550 g/1 lb 4 oz baby eels or
cleaned smelts or whitebait

COOK'S TIP

This is a very famous tapas dish
from the Basque country, usually
served with small wooden forks
to prevent people burning their
mouths. Baby eels are a seasonal
speciality and are now becoming
popular outside Spain. Smelts,
which resemble sardines in
appearance but are actually
members of the salmon family,
make good substitutes and you
could even use sprats.

1 Heat the olive oil in 4 individual,
flameproof earthenware dishes.
Stir in the garlic and chilli.

2 Add the eels and cook, stirring
frequently, for a few seconds.
If using smelts or whitebait, cook for a
further 2 minutes.

3 As soon as the dishes are sizzling
hot, serve immediately.

tuna rolls

serves four

3 red peppers

125 ml/4 fl oz olive oil

2 tbsp lemon juice

5 tbsp red wine vinegar

2 garlic cloves, finely chopped

1 tsp paprika

1 tsp dried chilli flakes

2 tsp sugar

2 tbsp salted capers

200 g/7 oz canned tuna in oil,
   drained and flaked

1 Preheat the grill to high. Place the peppers on a baking sheet and cook under the preheated grill, turning frequently, for 10 minutes, or until the skin is blackened and blistered all over. Using tongs, transfer to a polythene bag, tie the top and leave to cool.

2 Meanwhile, whisk the olive oil, lemon juice, vinegar, garlic, paprika, chilli flakes and sugar together in a small bowl.

3 When the peppers are cool enough to handle, peel off the skins, then cut the flesh into thirds lengthways and deseed. Place the pepper pieces in a non-metallic dish and pour over the dressing, turning to coat. Leave to stand in a cool place for 30 minutes.

4 Rub the salt off the capers and mix with the tuna. Drain the pepper pieces, reserving the dressing. Divide the tuna mixture between the pepper pieces and roll up. Secure with a wooden cocktail stick. Place the tuna rolls on a serving platter, spoon over the dressing and serve at room temperature.

tuna, egg & potato salad

serves four

350 g/12 oz new potatoes,
  unpeeled

1 hard-boiled egg, cooled
  and shelled

3 tbsp olive oil

1½ tbsp white wine vinegar

115 g/4 oz canned tuna in oil,
  drained and flaked

2 shallots, finely chopped

1 tomato, peeled and diced

2 tbsp chopped fresh parsley

salt and pepper

VARIATION

This salad is even more delicious
if it is made with fresh tuna that
has been griddled for 2 minutes
on each side, then diced.

1 Cook the potatoes in a saucepan of lightly salted boiling water for 10 minutes, then remove from the heat, cover and leave to stand for 15–20 minutes, or until tender.

2 Meanwhile, slice the egg, then cut each slice in half. Whisk the olive oil and vinegar together in a bowl and season to taste with salt and pepper. Spoon a little of the vinaigrette into a serving dish to coat the base.

3 Drain the potatoes, peel and thinly slice. Place half the slices over the base of the dish, season to taste with salt, then top with half the tuna, half the egg slices and half the shallots. Pour over half the remaining dressing. Make a second layer with the remaining potato slices, tuna, egg and shallots, then pour over the remaining dressing.

4 Finally, top the salad with the tomato and parsley, cover with clingfilm and leave to stand in a cool place for 1–2 hours before serving.

tuna with pimiento-stuffed olives

serves six

2 fresh tuna steaks, weighing about
   250 g/9 oz in total and about
   2.5 cm/1 inch thick

5 tbsp Spanish olive oil

3 tbsp red wine vinegar

4 fresh thyme sprigs, plus extra
   to garnish

1 bay leaf

2 tbsp plain flour

1 onion, finely chopped

2 garlic cloves, finely chopped

85 g/3 oz pimiento-stuffed green
   olives, sliced

salt and pepper

crusty bread, to serve

1 Don't get caught out with this recipe – the tuna steaks need to be marinated, so remember to start preparing the dish the day before you are going to serve it. Remove the skin from the tuna steaks, then cut the steaks in half along the grain of the fish. Cut each half into 1-cm/½-inch thick slices against the grain.

2 Place 3 tablespoons of the olive oil and the vinegar in a large, shallow, non-metallic dish. Strip the leaves from the thyme sprigs and add these to the dish with the bay leaf and salt and pepper to taste. Add the prepared strips of tuna, cover the dish and leave to marinate in the refrigerator for 8 hours or overnight.

3 The next day, place the flour in a polythene bag. Remove the tuna strips from the marinade, reserving the marinade for later, add them to the bag of flour and toss well until they are lightly coated in the flour.

4 Heat the remaining olive oil in a large, heavy-based frying pan. Add the onion and garlic and gently fry for 5–10 minutes, or until softened and golden brown. Add the tuna strips to the pan and fry for 2–5 minutes, turning several times, until the fish becomes opaque. Add the reserved marinade and olives to the pan and cook for a further 1–2 minutes, stirring, until the fish is tender and the sauce has thickened.

5 Serve the tuna and olives piping hot, garnished with thyme sprigs. Accompany with chunks or slices of crusty bread for mopping up the sauce.

spicy deep-fried whitebait

serves four

115 g/4 oz plain flour

½ tsp cayenne pepper

½ tsp ground cumin

1 tsp paprika

pinch of salt

1.25 kg/2 lb 12 oz whitebait

vegetable oil, for deep-frying

lemon slices, to garnish

1 Mix the flour, cayenne, cumin, paprika and salt together in a large bowl, plate or tray.

2 Rinse the fish and pat dry with kitchen paper. Add the fish to the seasoned flour, a few at a time, tossing well to coat.

3 Heat the vegetable oil in a deep-fat fryer or large saucepan to 180–190°C/350–375°F, or until a cube of bread browns in 30 seconds. Deep-fry the fish, in batches, for 2–3 minutes, or until golden brown.

VARIATION

This is also a delicious way of cooking sardines. However, they should be scaled and cleaned before cooking, unlike whitebait.

COOK'S TIP

If using frozen whitebait – fresh is often difficult to find – make sure that they are thoroughly thawed before cooking.

4 Drain well on kitchen paper and keep warm while you cook the remaining batches. Serve on warmed serving plates, garnished with lemon slices.

calamari

serves six

450 g/1 lb prepared squid

plain flour, for coating

sunflower oil, for deep-frying

salt

lemon wedges, to garnish

Aïoli (see page 12), to serve

COOK'S TIP

If you need to prepare the squid yourself, hold the body in one hand and pull on the head and tentacles with the other. The body contents will come away and can be discarded. Cut off the tentacles just above the eyes and discard the head. Remove the ink sacs from the head (keep them for another dish, if desired). Finally, remove the backbone and peel off the thin, dark outer skin.

1 Slice the squid into 1-cm/½-inch rings and halve the tentacles if large. Rinse and dry well on kitchen paper so that they do not spit during cooking. Dust the squid rings with flour so that they are lightly coated. Do not season the flour, as Spanish cooks will tell you that seasoning squid with salt before cooking toughens it.

2 Heat the sunflower oil in a deep-fat fryer to 180–190°C/ 350–375°F, or until a cube of bread browns in 30 seconds. Carefully add the squid rings, in batches so that the temperature of the oil does not drop. Deep-fry for 2–3 minutes, or until golden brown and crisp all over, turning several times. Do not overcook as the squid will become tough and rubbery rather than moist and tender.

3 Using a slotted spoon, remove the fried squid from the deep-fat fryer and drain well on kitchen paper. Keep warm in a warm oven while you deep-fry the remaining squid rings.

4 Sprinkle the deep-fried squid rings with salt and serve piping hot, garnished with lemon wedges for squeezing over them. Accompany with a bowl of Aïoli for dipping.

squid & cherry tomatoes

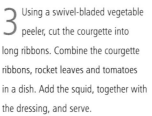

serves six

500 g/1 lb 2 oz prepared squid

7 tbsp olive oil

2 tbsp lemon juice

1 garlic clove, finely chopped

2 tbsp chopped fresh parsley

1 tbsp chopped fresh marjoram

pinch of cayenne pepper

1 courgette

1 bunch of rocket, separated
   into leaves

350 g/12 oz cherry tomatoes

1 Cut the squid into rings 1 cm/
½ inch thick. Heat 2 tablespoons
of the olive oil in a large, heavy-based
frying pan. Add the squid rings and
cook over a high heat, stirring
constantly, for 3 minutes, or until the
flesh becomes opaque and feels tender
when pierced with the point of a sharp
knife. Using a slotted spoon, transfer
the squid to a non-metallic bowl.

2 Whisk the remaining oil, the
lemon juice, garlic, parsley,
marjoram and cayenne together in a
bowl, then pour the dressing over the
squid. Toss well to coat, cover with
clingfilm and leave to cool. Chill for
up to 8 hours.

3 Using a swivel-bladed vegetable
peeler, cut the courgette into
long ribbons. Combine the courgette
ribbons, rocket leaves and tomatoes
in a dish. Add the squid, together with
the dressing, and serve.

COOK'S TIP

You can use fresh or thawed
frozen squid for this dish. The
secret is to cook it very briefly so
that it does not become tough.

stuffed squid in their own ink

serves six–eight

60 baby squid or 30 medium squid

150 ml/5 fl oz olive oil

100 ml/3½ fl oz white wine

4 Spanish onions, chopped

1 garlic bulb, separated into cloves
   and peeled

2 green peppers, deseeded
   and chopped

2 tomatoes, thinly sliced

100 ml/3½ fl oz red wine

100 ml/3½ fl oz water

salt and pepper

snipped fresh chives, to garnish

1 Partially fill a bowl with cold water. Clean each squid by gently pulling off the head. The insides will come away at the same time. Remove and reserve the ink sacs in the bowl of water. Cut off the tentacles from the heads, squeeze out and discard the beaks, scrape off the suckers with a sharp knife, then chop. Rinse the bodies and rub off the skin. Stuff the body sacs with the tentacles.

2 Heat 4 tablespoons of the olive oil in a large, heavy-based frying pan. Season the squid to taste with salt. Add to the pan, cover and cook, in batches if necessary, over a low heat, turning occasionally, for 5 minutes, or until golden brown all over. Drain well and reserve. Add more oil to the frying pan as required.

3 Pour the bowl of ink sacs into a food processor or blender, add the white wine and process until combined. Reserve.

4 Heat 4 tablespoons of the remaining oil in a separate frying pan. Add the onions and cook over a low heat, stirring occasionally, for 5 minutes. Add the garlic and green peppers, cover and cook for 15–20 minutes, or until the vegetables are very soft but not browned. Stir in the tomatoes, then pour in the ink mixture. Transfer the contents of the pan to the food processor or blender.

5 Add the squid to the frying pan, turning to coat in the mixture remaining on the base of the pan, then transfer to a flameproof casserole dish. Pour the red wine into the frying pan, add the water and cook over a low heat, scraping up the sediment from the base of the pan with a wooden spoon. Pour this mixture into the food processor or blender and process until combined. Press the sauce through a sieve, then pour it over the squid.

6 Cover the casserole dish and cook the squid in the sauce over a low heat for 1 hour. Serve immediately, sprinkled with the chives, or set aside until required and reheat gently before serving.

squid & beans

serves six

500 g/1 lb 2 oz prepared squid

3 garlic cloves, chopped

300 ml/10 fl oz dry red wine

500 g/1 lb 2 oz new potatoes,
    unpeeled

225 g/8 oz French beans, cut into
    short lengths

4 tbsp olive oil

1 tbsp red wine vinegar

salt and pepper

1 Preheat the oven to 180°C/350°F/
Gas Mark 4. Using a sharp knife,
cut the squid into rings about 1 cm/
½ inch thick and place them in an
ovenproof dish. Sprinkle with half the
garlic, pour over the wine and season
to taste with salt and pepper. Cover
the dish with foil and bake in the
preheated oven for 45–50 minutes,
or until the squid feels tender when
pierced with the point of a sharp knife.

2 Meanwhile, cook the potatoes
in a saucepan of lightly salted
boiling water for 15–20 minutes, or
until tender. Drain and leave to cool
slightly, then thickly slice and place
in a large bowl.

3 Cook the beans in a separate
saucepan of lightly salted boiling
water for 3–5 minutes, or until tender.
Drain and add to the potatoes. Drain
the squid and add to the bowl.

4 Whisk the olive oil, vinegar and
remaining garlic together in a
bowl and season to taste with salt and
pepper. Pour the dressing over the
salad and toss lightly. Divide the salad
between individual serving plates and
serve warm.

VARIATION

You can add 4 drained, sliced
sun-dried tomatoes in oil
and/or 2 tablespoons of pine
kernels to the potatoes with
the beans in Step 3.

crab with almonds

serves four

450 g/1 lb fresh, canned or frozen
  crabmeat, thawed
115 g/4 oz butter
85 g/3 oz flaked almonds
125 ml/4 fl oz double cream
1 tbsp chopped fresh parsley
salt and pepper

1 Pick over the crabmeat to remove any pieces of cartilage or shell. Melt half the butter in a heavy-based frying pan. Add the crabmeat and cook over a medium heat, stirring occasionally, for 10 minutes, or until browned. Remove the frying pan from the heat and reserve.

2 Melt the remaining butter in a separate frying pan. Add the almonds and cook over a low heat, stirring occasionally, for 5 minutes, or until golden brown.

3 Stir the almonds into the crabmeat and season to taste with salt and pepper. Stir in the cream and parsley and bring to the boil. Reduce the heat and simmer for 3 minutes. Transfer to a warmed serving dish and serve immediately.

COOK'S TIP

You can serve this with crusty bread or toast, or you can spoon it into ramekins or cleaned scallop shells and brown quickly under a preheated hot grill.

crab tartlets

makes twenty-four

1 tbsp Spanish olive oil

1 small onion, finely chopped

1 garlic clove, finely chopped

splash of dry white wine

2 eggs

150 ml/5 fl oz milk or single cream

175 g/6 oz canned crabmeat,
   drained

55 g/2 oz Manchego or Parmesan
   cheese, grated

2 tbsp chopped fresh
   flat-leaf parsley

pinch of freshly grated nutmeg

salt and pepper

fresh dill sprigs, to garnish

PASTRY

350 g/12 oz plain flour, plus extra
   for dusting

pinch of salt

175 g/6 oz butter

2 tbsp cold water

OR

500 g/1 lb 2 oz ready-made
   shortcrust pastry

1 Preheat the oven to 190°C/
375°F/Gas Mark 5. To prepare
the crabmeat filling, heat the olive oil
in a saucepan. Add the onion and fry
for 5 minutes, or until softened but
not browned. Add the garlic and fry
for a further 30 seconds. Add a splash
of the white wine and cook for
1–2 minutes, or until most of the wine
has evaporated.

2 Lightly whisk the eggs in a
large bowl, then whisk in the
milk or cream. Add the crabmeat,
grated cheese, parsley, and the onion
mixture. Season the mixture with
nutmeg and salt and pepper to taste
and mix together.

3 To prepare the pastry if you are
making it yourself, mix the flour
and salt together in a large bowl.
Add the butter, cut into small pieces,
and rub it in until the mixture
resembles fine breadcrumbs. Gradually

stir in enough of the water to form a
firm dough. Alternatively, the pastry
could be made in a food processor.

4 Thinly roll out the pastry on a
lightly floured work surface. Using
a plain, round 7-cm/2¾-inch cutter, cut
the pastry into 18 rounds. Gently pile
the trimmings together, roll out again,
then cut out a further 6 rounds. Use to
line 24 x 4-cm/1½-inch tartlet tins.
Carefully spoon the crabmeat mixture
into the pastry cases, taking care not to
overfill them.

5 Bake the tartlets in the preheated
oven for 25–30 minutes, or until
golden brown and set. Serve the
crab tartlets hot or cold, garnished with
fresh dill sprigs.

peppers stuffed with crab salad

makes sixteen

16 pimientos del piquillo, drained,
   or freshly roasted peppers, tops
   cut off (see Cook's Tip)
chopped fresh parsley, to garnish
CRAB SALAD
240 g/8½ oz canned crabmeat,
   drained and squeezed dry
1 red pepper, grilled, peeled (see
   page 74) and chopped
about 2 tbsp fresh lemon juice
200 g/7 oz cream cheese
salt and pepper

1 First make the crab salad. Pick over the crabmeat and remove any bits of shell. Put half the crabmeat in a food processor with the prepared red pepper, 1½ tablespoons of the lemon juice and salt and pepper to taste. Process until well blended, then transfer to a bowl. Flake and stir in the cream cheese and remaining crabmeat. Taste and add extra lemon juice, if required.

2 Pat the pimientos del piquillo dry and scoop out any seeds that remain in the tips. Use a small spoon to divide the crab salad equally between the peppers, stuffing them generously. Arrange on a large serving dish or individual plates, cover and leave to chill until required. Just before serving, sprinkle the stuffed peppers with the chopped parsley.

COOK'S TIP

If you can't find pimientos del piquillo, and have to roast the peppers yourself, use 16 of the long, sweet Mediterranean variety, not capsicums. If, however, capsicums are the only ones you can find, cut 4–6 into wedges and spread the crab salad along each wedge.

battered prawns & coriander dip

serves four

12 raw Mediterranean prawns

1 egg

125 ml/4 fl oz water

115 g/4 oz plain flour

1 tsp cayenne pepper

vegetable oil, for deep-frying

orange wedges, to garnish

CORIANDER DIP

1 large bunch of fresh coriander,
   roughly chopped

3 garlic cloves, chopped

2 tbsp tomato purée

2 tbsp lemon juice

1 tbsp grated lemon rind

1½ tbsp sugar

1 tsp ground cumin

5 tbsp olive oil

1 First make the coriander dip. Place the coriander, garlic, tomato purée, lemon juice, lemon rind, sugar and cumin in a food processor or blender and process until combined. With the motor still running, gradually add the olive oil through the feeder tube until fully incorporated. Scrape into a bowl, cover with clingfilm and leave to chill until required.

2 Pull the heads off the prawns and peel, leaving the tails intact. Cut along the length of the back of each prawn and remove and discard the dark vein. Rinse under cold running water, then pat dry with kitchen paper.

3 Whisk the egg with the water in a small bowl. Gradually sift in the flour and cayenne, whisking constantly until smooth.

4 Heat the vegetable oil in a deep-fat fryer or large saucepan to 180–190°C/350–375°F, or until a cube of bread browns in 30 seconds. Holding the prawns by their tails, dip them into the batter, one at a time, shaking off any excess. Add the prawns to the oil and deep-fry for 2–3 minutes, or until crisp. Remove with a slotted spoon and drain well on kitchen paper. Serve immediately, garnished with orange wedges. Hand round the coriander dip separately.

VARIATION

These battered prawns are also delicious served with Chilli Sauce (see page 11).

garlic prawns with lemon and parsley

serves six

60 raw tiger prawns, thawed if
   using frozen

150 ml/5 fl oz olive oil

6 garlic cloves, thinly sliced

3 dried hot red chillies (optional)

6 tbsp freshly squeezed lemon juice

6 tbsp very finely chopped
   fresh parsley

French bread, to serve

1 Peel and devein the prawns and remove the heads, leaving the tails on. Rinse and pat the prawns dry.

2 Heat the olive oil in a large, deep sauté pan or frying pan. Add the garlic and chillies, if using, and stir constantly until they begin to sizzle. Add the prawns and cook until they turn pink and begin to curl.

3 Use a slotted spoon to transfer the prawns to warm earthenware bowls. Sprinkle each bowl with lemon juice and parsley. Serve with plenty of bread to mop up the juices.

COOK'S TIP

To devein prawns, use a fine-bladed knife to slice along the back from the head end to the tail, then remove the thin, black intestine.

giant garlic prawns

serves four

125 ml/4 fl oz olive oil

4 garlic cloves, finely chopped

2 hot fresh red chillies, deseeded
and finely chopped

450 g/1 lb cooked tiger prawns

2 tbsp chopped fresh
flat-leaf parsley

salt and pepper

lemon wedges, to garnish

crusty bread, to serve

COOK'S TIP

If you use raw prawns, cook
them as above but increase the
cooking time to 5–6 minutes,
or until the prawns are cooked
through and turn bright pink. If
using frozen prawns, make sure
they are thoroughly thawed
before cooking.

1 Heat the olive oil in a preheated
wok or large, heavy-based
frying pan over a low heat. Add the
garlic and chillies and cook, stirring
occasionally, for 1–2 minutes, until
softened but not coloured.

2 Add the prawns and stir-fry for
2–3 minutes, or until heated
through and coated in the oil and
garlic mixture.

3 Turn off the heat and add the
chopped parsley, stirring well
to mix. Season to taste with salt
and pepper.

4 Divide the prawns and garlic-
flavoured oil between warmed
serving dishes and garnish with
lemon wedges. Serve with lots of
crusty bread.

lime-drizzled prawns

serves six

4 limes

12 raw tiger prawns, in their shells

3 tbsp Spanish olive oil

2 garlic cloves, finely chopped

splash of dry sherry

4 tbsp chopped fresh
   flat-leaf parsley

salt and pepper

1 Grate the rind and squeeze out the juice from 2 of the limes. Cut the remaining 2 limes into wedges and reserve until required.

2 To prepare the prawns, remove the legs, leaving the shells and tails intact. Cut along the length of the back of each prawn and remove the dark vein and discard. Rinse the prawns under cold running water and dry well on kitchen paper.

3 Heat the olive oil in a large, heavy-based frying pan, then add the garlic and fry for 30 seconds. Add the prawns and fry for 5 minutes, stirring occasionally, or until they turn pink and begin to curl. Mix in the lime rind, juice and a splash of sherry to moisten, then stir well together.

4 Transfer the cooked prawns to a serving dish, season to taste with salt and pepper and sprinkle over the chopped parsley.

5 Serve piping hot, accompanied by the reserved lime wedges for squeezing over the prawns.

prawns wrapped in ham

makes sixteen

16 raw tiger prawns

16 thin slices serrano ham
   or prosciutto

extra virgin olive oil

TOMATO-CAPER DRESSING

2 tomatoes, peeled and deseeded
   (see Cook's Tip)

1 small red onion, very
   finely chopped

4 tbsp very finely chopped
   fresh parsley

1 tbsp capers in brine, drained,
   rinsed and chopped

finely grated rind of 1 large lemon

4 tbsp extra virgin olive oil

1 tbsp sherry vinegar

COOK'S TIP

To peel and deseed tomatoes,
remove the stems and cut a cross
in the tops. Place them in a
heatproof bowl, pour over boiling
water to cover and leave for
30 seconds. Use a slotted spoon
to transfer to a bowl of iced
water. Peel off the skin, then cut
in half and scoop out the
cores and seeds.

1 Preheat the oven to 160°C/
325°F/Gas Mark 3. To make
the dressing, finely chop the prepared
tomato flesh and place in a bowl.
Add the onion, parsley, capers and
lemon rind and gently toss together.
Combine the olive oil and vinegar and
add to the other ingredients. Reserve
until required.

2 Pull the heads off the prawns
and peel, leaving the tails intact.
Cut along the length of the back of
each prawn and remove and discard
the dark vein. Rinse and pat dry. Wrap
a slice of ham around each prawn and
rub with a little oil. Place the prawns
in a heatproof dish large enough to
hold them in a single layer. Bake in
the preheated oven for 10 minutes.

3 Transfer the prawns to a serving
platter and spoon the dressing
over. Serve immediately, or leave to
cool to room temperature.

prawns with saffron dressing

serves six–eight

large pinch of saffron threads

2 tbsp warm water

150 ml/5 fl oz mayonnaise

2 tbsp grated onion

4 tbsp lemon juice

1 tsp Dijon mustard

1 kg/2 lb 4 oz cooked

    Mediterranean prawns

1 cos lettuce, separated

    into leaves

4 tomatoes, cut into wedges

8 black olives

salt and pepper

1 Stir the saffron with the water in a small bowl. Mix the mayonnaise, onion, lemon juice and mustard together in a separate, non-metallic bowl, whisking gently until thoroughly combined. Season to taste with salt and pepper and stir in the saffron soaking liquid. Cover with clingfilm and leave to chill until required.

2 Pull the heads off the prawns and peel. Cut along the length of the back of each prawn and remove and discard the dark vein. Rinse and pat dry with kitchen paper.

3 Arrange the lettuce leaves on a large serving platter or on individual serving plates. Top with the prawns and scatter with the tomato wedges and olives. Serve with the saffron dressing.

spicy prawns in sherry

serves four

12 raw Mediterranean prawns

2 tbsp olive oil

2 tbsp dry sherry

pinch of cayenne pepper or dash of
Tabasco sauce

salt and pepper

1 Pull the heads off the prawns and peel, leaving the tails intact. Cut along the length of the back of each prawn and remove and discard the dark vein. Rinse and pat dry.

2 Heat the olive oil in a large, heavy-based frying pan. Add the prawns and cook over a medium heat, stirring occasionally, for 2–3 minutes, or until they have turned pink. Add the sherry and season to taste with cayenne, salt and pepper.

3 Tip the contents of the frying pan onto a serving platter. Impale each prawn with a wooden cocktail stick and serve.

saffron prawns with lemon mayonnaise

serves six–eight

1.25 kg/2 lb 12 oz raw
  Mediterranean prawns
85 g/3 oz plain flour
125 ml/4 fl oz light beer
2 tbsp olive oil
pinch of saffron powder
2 egg whites
vegetable oil, for deep-frying
LEMON MAYONNAISE
4 garlic cloves
2 egg yolks
1 tbsp lemon juice
1 tbsp finely grated lemon rind
300 ml/10 fl oz sunflower oil
sea salt and pepper

1 First make the mayonnaise. Place the garlic cloves on a chopping board and sprinkle with a little sea salt, then flatten them with the side of a heavy knife. Finely chop and flatten again.

COOK'S TIP

This mayonnaise goes well with all kinds of fried fish and seafood. Try it with squid, sardines or deep-fried mussels.

2 Transfer the garlic to a food processor or blender and add the egg yolks, lemon juice and lemon rind. Process briefly until just blended. With the motor still running, gradually add the sunflower oil through the feeder tube until it is fully incorporated. Scrape the mayonnaise into a serving bowl, season to taste with salt and pepper, then cover and leave to chill until required.

3 Pull the heads off the prawns and peel, leaving the tails intact. Cut along the length of the back of each prawn and remove and discard the dark vein. Rinse under cold running water and pat dry with kitchen paper.

4 Sift the flour into a bowl. Mix the beer, oil and saffron together in a jug, then gradually whisk into the flour. Cover and leave at room temperature for 30 minutes to rest.

5 Whisk the egg whites in a spotlessly clean, greasefree bowl until stiff. Gently fold the egg whites into the flour mixture.

6 Heat the vegetable oil in a deep-fat fryer or large saucepan to 180–190°C/350–375°F, or until a cube of bread browns in 30 seconds. Holding the prawns by their tails, dip them into the batter and shake off any excess. Add the prawns to the oil and deep-fry for 2–3 minutes, or until crisp. Remove with a slotted spoon and drain well on kitchen paper. Serve immediately with the mayonnaise.

prawn rissoles

serves eight–ten

250 g/9 oz plain flour, plus extra
   for dusting
250 g/9 oz butter
150 ml/5 fl oz iced water
1 tsp lemon juice
225 ml/8 fl oz milk
freshly grated nutmeg
1 bay leaf
450 g/1 lb cooked peeled prawns
1 hard-boiled egg, cooled, shelled
   and chopped
1 tbsp paprika
pinch of cayenne pepper
1 tbsp chopped fresh parsley
vegetable oil, for deep-frying
salt and pepper

1 Sift 225 g/8 oz of the flour with a pinch of salt into a bowl. Add 55 g/2 oz of the butter and rub it in until the mixture resembles breadcrumbs. Stir in the water and lemon juice and mix to a dough. Knead lightly, then shape into a ball, cover and chill for 15 minutes. Place 175 g/6 oz of the remaining butter between 2 sheets of greaseproof paper and beat out into a rectangle 5 mm/¼ inch thick.

2 Roll out the dough on a lightly floured work surface into a rectangle 5 mm/¼ inch thick. Place the butter rectangle in the centre. Fold the top and bottom of the dough over it, wrap in foil and leave to chill for 10 minutes.

3 Place the dough on a lightly floured work surface with a folded edge facing you. Roll out to about 5 mm/¼ inch thick, then fold into 3 again, wrap and leave to chill for 15 minutes. Repeat rolling and folding twice more.

4 Meanwhile, melt the remaining butter in a saucepan. Add the remaining flour and cook, stirring constantly, for 2 minutes, or until golden. Remove from the heat and gradually stir in the milk. Return to the heat and bring to the boil, stirring constantly until thickened and smooth. Reduce the heat to very low, season

to taste with salt, pepper and nutmeg and add the bay leaf. Remove from the heat and leave to cool.

5 Mix the prawns and egg together in a bowl, then fold in the sauce, removing and discarding the bay leaf. Stir in the paprika, cayenne and parsley.

6 Roll out the dough to a rectangle about 5 mm/¼ inch thick and cut into 7.5-cm/3-inch squares. Place 1 teaspoon of the prawn mixture on each square. Brush the edges with water and fold the dough over to make triangles, pressing the edges to seal.

7 Heat the vegetable oil in a deep-fat fryer or large saucepan to 180–190°C/350–375°F, or until a cube of bread browns in 30 seconds. Deep-fry the dough triangles, in batches, for 2 minutes, or until golden and puffed up. Remove with a slotted spoon and drain on kitchen paper. Serve hot.

sizzling chilli prawns

serves six

500 g/1 lb 2 oz raw tiger prawns,
  in their shells

1 small fresh red chilli

6 tbsp Spanish olive oil

2 garlic cloves, finely chopped

pinch of paprika

salt

crusty bread, to serve

1 Pull the heads off the prawns and peel, leaving the tails intact. Cut along the length of the back of each prawn and remove and discard the dark vein. Rinse the prawns under cold running water and pat dry on kitchen paper.

2 Cut the chilli in half lengthways, remove the seeds and finely chop the flesh.

3 Heat the olive oil in a large, heavy-based frying pan or flameproof casserole until quite hot, then add the garlic and fry for 30 seconds. Add the prawns, chilli, paprika and a pinch of salt and fry for 2–3 minutes, stirring constantly, until the prawns turn pink and begin to curl.

4 Serve the prawns in the cooking dish, still sizzling. Accompany with wooden cocktail sticks, to spear the prawns, and chunks or slices of crusty bread to mop up the aromatic cooking oil.

> ### COOK'S TIP
> It is important either to wear gloves or to wash your hands very thoroughly after chopping chillies as their juices can cause irritation to sensitive skin, especially around the eyes, nose or mouth. You should never rub your eyes after touching the cut flesh of the chilli.

cidered scallops

serves four–five

1 litre/1¾ pints dry cider

4 tbsp lemon juice

20 shelled scallops

85 g/3 oz butter

25 g/1 oz plain flour

225 ml/8 fl oz soured cream

115 g/4 oz button mushrooms

salt and pepper

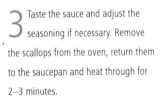

COOK'S TIP

Although we usually think of wine and sherry in relation to Spain, the country produces quite large quantities of *sidra*, or cider, which is popular for cooking seafood as well as for drinking.

1 Preheat the oven to 110°C/225°F/ Gas Mark ¼. Pour the cider and lemon juice into a large, shallow saucepan and season to taste with salt and pepper. Add the scallops and poach for 10 minutes, or until tender. Using a slotted spoon, transfer the scallops to an ovenproof dish. Dot with 25 g/1 oz of the butter, cover with foil and keep warm in the oven.

2 Bring the scallop cooking liquid to the boil and continue to boil until reduced by about half. Mix together 25 g/1 oz of the remaining butter and the flour, mashing well with a fork to make a paste. Beat the paste, a little at a time, into the liquid until thickened and smooth. Stir in the soured cream and simmer gently for 5–10 minutes.

3 Taste the sauce and adjust the seasoning if necessary. Remove the scallops from the oven, return them to the saucepan and heat through for 2–3 minutes.

4 Meanwhile, melt the remaining butter in a small frying pan. Add the mushrooms and cook over a low heat, stirring frequently, for 2–3 minutes. Add them to the saucepan of scallops, then transfer to individual serving dishes and serve.

scallops with serrano ham

serves four

2 tbsp lemon juice

3 tbsp olive oil

2 garlic cloves, finely chopped

1 tbsp chopped fresh parsley

12 shelled scallops, preferably
  with corals

16 wafer-thin slices serrano ham

pepper

1 Mix the lemon juice, olive oil, garlic and parsley together in a non-metallic dish. Separate the corals, if using, from the scallops and add both to the dish, turning to coat. Cover with clingfilm and leave to marinate at room temperature for 20 minutes.

2 Preheat the grill to medium. Drain the scallops, reserving the marinade. Scrunch up a slice of ham and thread it onto a metal skewer, followed by a scallop and a coral, if using. Repeat to fill 4 skewers each with the ham, scallops and corals, and finishing with a scrunched-up slice of ham.

3 Cook under the hot grill, basting generously with the marinade and turning frequently, for 5 minutes, or until the scallops are tender and the ham is crisp.

4 Transfer to warmed serving plates, sprinkle them with pepper, spoon over the cooking juices from the grill pan and serve.

COOK'S TIP

Although bottled lemon juice is a useful refrigerator stand-by, freshly squeezed juice always has more flavour. Make sure citrus fruit is at room temperature for maximum juice yield. It also helps if you roll the fruit backwards and forwards over a work surface a couple of times before squeezing.

seared scallops

serves four–six

4 tbsp olive oil

3 tbsp orange juice

2 tsp hazelnut oil

24 shelled scallops

salad leaves (optional)

175 g/6 oz Cabrales or other blue
   cheese, crumbled

2 tbsp chopped fresh dill

salt and pepper

1 Whisk 3 tablespoons of the olive
oil, the orange juice and hazelnut
oil together in a jug and season to
taste with salt and pepper.

2 Heat the remaining olive oil in a
large, heavy-based frying pan.
Add the scallops and cook over a high
heat for 1 minute on each side, or
until golden.

3 Transfer the scallops to a bed of
salad leaves or individual plates.
Scatter over the cheese and dill, then
drizzle with the dressing. Serve warm.

COOK'S TIP

If you are using fresh scallops
in their shells, the easiest way
to prepare them is to place the
shells, rounded-side down,
on an electric hob or in a low
oven at about 150°C/300°F/
Gas Mark 2 for a few minutes
first. The shells will open slightly,
making it much easier to insert a
knife blade to prise them apart
and slice the white muscle off the
bottom of the shell.

scallops in orange juice

serves six

plain flour, for dusting

30 shelled scallops, preferably
     with corals

4 tbsp olive oil

100 ml/3½ fl oz freshly squeezed
     orange juice

salt and pepper

fresh parsley sprigs, to garnish

1 Spread out the flour on a shallow plate. Add the scallops, a few at a time, and turn to coat well. Shake off any excess flour.

2 Heat the olive oil in a large, heavy-based frying pan. Add the scallops and cook, turning once, for 2 minutes, or until tender. Season to taste with salt and pepper, add the orange juice and cook for a further 2 minutes.

3 Transfer to warmed serving plates and serve immediately, garnished with parsley sprigs.

COOK'S TIP

If using frozen scallops, make sure that they are thoroughly thawed before cooking, but fresh scallops are much tastier. Do not overcook, which is easily done, or they will be tough.

scallops in saffron sauce

serves eight

150 ml/5 fl oz dry white wine

150 ml/5 fl oz fish stock

large pinch of saffron threads

900 g/2 lb shelled scallops,
    preferably large ones

3 tbsp Spanish olive oil

1 small onion, finely chopped

2 garlic cloves, finely chopped

150 ml/5 fl oz double cream

squeeze of lemon juice

salt and pepper

chopped fresh flat-leaf parsley,
    plus extra sprigs, to garnish

crusty bread, to serve

1 Place the wine, fish stock and saffron in a saucepan and bring to the boil. Reduce the heat, cover and simmer gently for 15 minutes.

2 Meanwhile, remove and discard from each scallop the tough, white muscle that is found opposite the coral, and separate the coral from the scallop. Slice the scallops vertically into thick slices, including the corals if they are present. Dry the scallops well on kitchen paper, then season to taste.

3 Heat the olive oil in a large, heavy-based frying pan. Add the onion and garlic and fry for 5 minutes, or until softened and lightly browned. Add the sliced scallops to the pan and fry gently for 5 minutes, stirring occasionally, or until they just turn opaque. The secret is not to overcook the scallops, otherwise they will become tough and rubbery.

4 Using a slotted spoon, remove the scallops from the frying pan and transfer to a warmed plate. Add the saffron liquid to the pan, bring to the boil and boil rapidly until reduced to about half. Reduce the heat and gradually stir in the cream, just a little at a time. Simmer gently until the sauce thickens.

5 Return the scallops to the frying pan and simmer for 1–2 minutes just to heat them through. Add a squeeze of lemon juice and season to taste with salt and pepper. Serve the scallops hot, garnished with the parsley and accompanied by chunks or slices of crusty bread to mop up the saffron sauce.

baked scallops

serves four

700 g/1 lb 9 oz shelled scallops, chopped

2 onions, finely chopped

2 garlic cloves, finely chopped

3 tbsp chopped fresh parsley

pinch of freshly grated nutmeg

pinch of ground cloves

2 tbsp fresh white breadcrumbs

2 tbsp olive oil

salt and pepper

COOK'S TIP

This looks particularly pretty served in scallop shells; you can usually obtain them from a good fishmonger. It is an especially appropriate way to serve this tapa, which comes from the pilgrimage town of Santiago de Compostela, dedicated to St James whose symbol is a scallop shell.

1 Preheat the oven to 200°C/ 400°F/Gas Mark 6. Mix the scallops, onions, garlic, 2 tablespoons of the parsley, the nutmeg and cloves together in a bowl and season to taste with salt and pepper.

2 Divide the mixture between 4 scrubbed scallop shells or heatproof dishes. Sprinkle the breadcrumbs and remaining parsley on top and drizzle with the olive oil.

3 Bake the scallops in the preheated oven for 15– 20 minutes, or until lightly golden and piping hot. Serve immediately.

catalan mussels

serves four

2 kg/4 lb 8 oz live mussels,
   scrubbed and debearded
5 tbsp olive oil
2 onions, chopped
2 garlic cloves, finely chopped
4 large tomatoes, peeled,
   deseeded (see page 167)
   and finely chopped
1 bay leaf
1 tbsp brandy
½ tsp paprika
salt and pepper
crusty bread, to serve

COOK'S TIP

When buying mussels, choose
ones that have a fresh, salty
smell and undamaged shells. Do
not pick any mussels that are
heavy, as they may be full of
sand, or any that feel very light,
as they may be dead.

1 Discard any mussels with broken or damaged shells and any that do not shut immediately when sharply tapped with the back of a knife.

2 Heat the olive oil in a large, heavy-based saucepan or flameproof casserole. Add the onion and garlic and cook over a low heat, stirring occasionally, for 5 minutes, or until softened. Add the tomatoes and bay leaf and cook, stirring occasionally, for a further 5 minutes.

3 Stir in the brandy and paprika and season to taste with salt and pepper. Increase the heat, add the mussels, cover the saucepan and cook, shaking the saucepan occasionally, for 5 minutes, or until the shells have opened. Discard the bay leaf and any mussels that have not opened. Transfer the mussels to a warmed serving dish and pour the sauce over them. Serve immediately with crusty bread or leave to cool.

golden mussels

serves four–six

500 g/1 lb 2 oz live mussels

about 175 ml/6 fl oz water

4 tbsp olive oil

1 garlic clove, finely chopped

2 tbsp chopped fresh parsley

40 g/1½ oz fresh white
  breadcrumbs

1 tomato, peeled, deseeded
  (see page 167) and chopped

1 Scrub the mussels under cold running water and pull out any beards that are attached to them. Discard any mussels with broken shells or any that do not close immediately when sharply tapped with the back of a knife.

2 Place the mussels in a large saucepan and add the water. Bring to the boil, cover and cook over a high heat, shaking the saucepan occasionally, for 3–5 minutes, or until the mussels have opened. Discard any that remain closed.

3 Discard the empty half shells. Remove the mussels from the other half shells. Reserving these shells, mix the mussels, olive oil, garlic and parsley together in a bowl, cover with clingfilm and chill for 30 minutes.

COOK'S TIP

The somewhat larger Spanish mussels with mottled brown shells are ideal for this recipe, but if you can't find them, the smaller black-shelled variety is fine.

4 Preheat the oven to 220°C/ 425°F/Gas Mark 7. Mix the breadcrumbs and tomato together in a separate bowl. Return the mussels to the reserved half-shells and place in an ovenproof dish in a single layer. Spoon the breadcrumb mixture over the mussels and bake in the preheated oven for 5 minutes, or until hot and golden brown. Serve immediately.

chilli-marinated mussels

serves six–eight

1 kg/2 lb 4 oz live mussels

1 lemon, sliced

2 garlic cloves, finely chopped

175 ml/6 fl oz white wine

125 ml/4 fl oz olive oil

3 tbsp lemon juice

1 tbsp Dijon mustard

2 tsp sugar

1 fresh red chilli, deseeded and
finely chopped

2 tbsp chopped fresh parsley

1 tbsp capers in brine, drained
and chopped

rock salt or crushed ice, to serve
(optional)

VARIATION

For a luxurious treat, you can prepare this tapa with oysters (far less expensive in Spain). For the initial cooking, open the oysters and remove from the shells. Place them in a saucepan and strain in the liquid from the shells. Poach gently until tender, then proceed according to the recipe.

1 Scrub the mussels under cold running water and pull out any beards that are attached to them. Discard any mussels with broken shells or any that do not close immediately when sharply tapped with the back of a knife.

2 Place the lemon slices and garlic in a large, heavy-based saucepan, pour in the wine and bring to the boil. Add the mussels, cover and cook over a high heat, shaking the saucepan occasionally, for 3–5 minutes, or until the mussels have opened. Discard any that remain closed.

3 Discard the empty half-shells. Remove the mussels from the other half-shells, reserving these half-shells. Mix the olive oil, lemon juice, mustard, sugar, chilli, parsley and capers together in a large, non-metallic bowl. Add the mussels and toss well to coat. Cover with clingfilm and leave to marinate in the refrigerator for up to 24 hours.

4 To serve, return the mussels to the reserved half-shells and arrange on a bed of rock salt or crushed ice on a serving platter, if you like. Spoon the marinade over the mussels and serve.

mussels with garlic butter

serves eight

800 g/1 lb 12 oz live mussels,
in their shells

splash of dry white wine

1 bay leaf

85 g/3 oz butter

350 g/12 oz fresh white or brown
breadcrumbs

4 tbsp chopped fresh flat-leaf
parsley, plus extra sprigs
to garnish

2 tbsp snipped fresh chives

2 garlic cloves, finely chopped

salt and pepper

lemon wedges, to serve

1 Clean the mussels by scrubbing or scraping the shells and pulling out any beards that are attached to them. Discard any with broken shells and any that refuse to close when sharply tapped with the back of a knife. Place the mussels in a colander and rinse under cold running water.

2 Place the mussels in a large saucepan and add a splash of wine and the bay leaf. Cook, covered, over a high heat for 5 minutes, shaking the saucepan occasionally, or until the mussels are opened. Drain the mussels and discard any that remain closed.

3 Shell the mussels, reserving one half of each shell. Arrange the mussels, in their half-shells, in a large, shallow, ovenproof serving dish.

4 Melt the butter and pour into a bowl. Add the breadcrumbs, parsley, chives, garlic and salt and pepper to taste and mix well together. Leave until the butter has set slightly. Using your fingers or 2 teaspoons, take a large pinch of the herb and butter mixture and use to fill each mussel shell, pressing it down well. Leave the mussels to chill until ready to serve.

5 To serve, preheat the oven to 230°C/450°F/Gas Mark 8. Bake the mussels in the preheated oven for 10 minutes, or until hot. Serve immediately, garnished with parsley sprigs and accompanied by lemon wedges for squeezing over them.

deep-fried mussels with a chilli dressing

serves six–eight

4 tbsp olive oil

2 tbsp white wine vinegar

1 tbsp chopped fresh parsley

1–2 fresh red chillies, deseeded and
finely chopped

1 fresh green chilli, deseeded and
finely chopped

½ tsp sugar

1 kg/2 lb 4 oz live mussels

about 175 ml/6 fl oz water

55 g/2 oz instant polenta

vegetable oil, for deep-frying

1 Mix the olive oil, vinegar, parsley, chillies and sugar together in a bowl. Cover with clingfilm and leave to chill until required.

2 Scrub the mussels under cold running water and pull out any beards that are attached to them. Discard any mussels with broken shells or any that do not close immediately when sharply tapped with the back of a knife.

3 Place the mussels in a large saucepan and add the water. Bring to the boil, cover and cook over a high heat, shaking the saucepan occasionally, for 3–5 minutes, or until the mussels have opened. Discard any that remain closed.

4 Remove the mussels from the shells, discarding the shells. Spread out the polenta on a shallow plate. Toss the mussels, a few at a time, in the polenta to coat, shaking off any excess.

5 Heat the vegetable oil in a deep-fat fryer or large saucepan to 180–190°C/350–375°F, or until a cube of bread browns in 30 seconds. Deep-fry the mussels, in batches if necessary, for a few minutes until golden brown. Drain on kitchen paper and serve hot with the dressing.

mussels with yellow pepper sauce

serves four–six

½ cucumber, peeled and
  halved lengthways

2 onions, chopped

2 tbsp chopped fresh parsley

1 yellow pepper, deseeded
  and chopped

1 fresh red chilli, deseeded
  and chopped

150 ml/5 fl oz dry white wine

2 tbsp olive oil

1 tbsp lemon juice

500 g/1 lb 2 oz live mussels

salt and pepper

COOK'S TIP

Serve these mussels as part of
a seafood tapa with Saffron
Prawns with Lemon Mayonnaise
(see page 170), Tuna Rolls (see
page 146), Scallops with Serrano
Ham (see page 176) and fresh
raw oysters on the half shell,
sprinkled with pepper.

Discard any mussels with broken shells
or any that do not close immediately
when sharply tapped with the back
of a knife.

1 Scoop out the seeds from the cucumber using a teaspoon, then finely chop the flesh. Mix the cucumber, half the onion, half the parsley, the yellow pepper and chilli together in a non-metallic bowl and season to taste with salt and pepper. Whisk in 2 tablespoons of the wine, the olive oil and lemon juice. Cover with clingfilm and leave to stand at room temperature for 30 minutes.

2 Scrub the mussels under cold running water and pull out any beards that are attached to them.

3 Pour the remaining wine into a large, heavy-based saucepan and add the remaining onion and parsley. Bring to the boil and add the mussels. Cover and cook over a high heat, shaking the saucepan occasionally, for 3–5 minutes, or until the mussels have opened. Discard any that remain closed.

4 Discard the empty half-shells. Place the mussels, in the remaining half-shells, on serving plates. Spoon the sauce over them and serve.

almejas a la plancha

serves four–six

500 g/1 lb 2 oz fresh carpet-shell or
other medium-sized clams

olive oil, for brushing and drizzling

lemon wedges, to garnish

COOK'S TIP

In Spain, razor clams are often
cooked in this wonderfully
delicious yet simple way.
Unfortunately, they are not
widely available commercially
elsewhere, but if you find them,
they are worth buying.
Griddle them hinge-side down
until they open, then turn and
cook as described.

---

1 Scrub the clams under cold
running water. Discard any with
broken shells or any that do not close
immediately when sharply tapped with
the back of a knife.

2 Heat a griddle pan over a high
heat, then brush with olive oil.
Add the clams in a single layer. As
soon as they have opened, turn them
over so that they are flesh-side down
and cook for 2 minutes.

3 Turn the clams again and drizzle
with a little more oil. Transfer to a
serving platter and pour over the
griddle pan juices. Garnish with lemon
wedges and serve immediately.

clams with broad beans

serves four–six

4 canned anchovy fillets in oil,
   drained

1 tsp salted capers

3 tbsp olive oil

1 tbsp sherry vinegar

1 tsp Dijon mustard

500 g/1 lb 2 oz fresh clams

about 175 ml/6 fl oz water

500 g/1 lb 2 oz broad beans,
   shelled if fresh

2 tbsp chopped mixed fresh herbs,
   such as parsley, chives and mint

salt and pepper

1 Place the anchovies in a small bowl, add water to cover and leave to soak for 5 minutes. Drain well, pat dry with kitchen paper and place in a mortar. Brush the salt off the capers, add to the mortar and pound to a paste with a pestle.

2 Whisk the olive oil, vinegar and mustard together in a separate bowl, then whisk in the anchovy paste and season to taste with salt and pepper. Cover with clingfilm and leave to stand at room temperature until required.

3 Scrub the clams under cold running water. Discard any with broken shells or any that do not close immediately when sharply tapped with the back of a knife. Place the clams in a large, heavy-based saucepan and add the water. Cover and bring to the boil over a high heat. Cook, shaking the pan occasionally, for 3–5 minutes, or until the clams have opened. Discard any that remain closed.

4 Meanwhile, bring a large saucepan of lightly salted water to the boil. Add the broad beans, return to the boil and blanch for 5 minutes. Drain, refresh under cold running water and drain well again. Remove and discard the outer skins and place the broad beans in a bowl.

5 Drain the clams and remove them from their shells. Add to the beans and sprinkle with the herbs. Add the anchovy vinaigrette and toss lightly. Serve warm.

clams in tomato & garlic sauce

serves six–eight

2 hard-boiled eggs, cooled, shelled
and halved lengthways

3 tbsp olive oil

1 Spanish onion, chopped

2 garlic cloves, finely chopped

700 g/1 lb 9 oz tomatoes, peeled
and diced

40 g/1½ oz fresh white
breadcrumbs

1 kg/2 lb 4 oz fresh clams

425 ml/15 fl oz dry white wine

2 tbsp chopped fresh parsley

salt and pepper

lemon wedges, to garnish

1 Scoop out the egg yolks using a teaspoon and rub through a fine sieve into a bowl. Chop the whites and reserve separately.

2 Heat the olive oil in a large, heavy-based frying pan. Add the onion and cook over a low heat, stirring occasionally, for 5 minutes, or until softened. Add the garlic and cook for a further 3 minutes, then add the tomatoes, breadcrumbs and egg yolks and season to taste with salt and pepper. Cook, stirring occasionally and mashing the mixture with a wooden spoon, for a further 10–15 minutes, or until thick and pulpy.

3 Meanwhile, scrub the clams under cold running water. Discard any with broken shells or any that do not close immediately when sharply tapped with the back of a knife.

4 Place the clams in a large, heavy-based saucepan. Add the wine and bring to the boil. Cover and cook over a high heat, shaking the saucepan occasionally, for 3–5 minutes, or until the clams have opened. Discard any that remain closed.

5 Using a slotted spoon, transfer the clams to warmed serving bowls. Strain the cooking liquid into the tomato sauce, stir well and spoon over the clams. Sprinkle with the chopped egg whites and parsley and serve immediately, garnished with lemon wedges.

oysters with sherry vinegar

serves four

1 shallot, finely chopped

3 tbsp sherry vinegar

3 tbsp red wine vinegar

1 tbsp sugar

24 fresh oysters

rock salt or crushed ice, to serve
    (optional)

pepper

1 Mix the shallot, vinegars and sugar together in a non-metallic bowl and season well with pepper. Cover with clingfilm and leave to stand at room temperature for at least 15 minutes to allow the flavours to mingle.

2 Meanwhile, shuck the oysters. Wrap a tea towel around your hand to protect it and hold an oyster firmly. Insert an oyster knife or other strong, sharp knife into the hinged edge and twist to prise the shells apart. Still holding both shells firmly in the wrapped hand, slide the blade of the knife along the upper shell to sever the muscle. Lift off the upper shell, being careful not to spill the liquid inside. Slide the blade of the knife along the lower shell underneath the oyster to sever the second muscle. Arrange the oysters on their half-shells in a single layer on a bed of rock salt or crushed ice, if you like.

3 Spoon the dressing evenly over the oysters and serve at room temperature.

COOK'S TIP

Many fishmongers are happy to shuck oysters for you. However, it is difficult to retain the 'liquor' in the shells. They should be eaten on the day of purchase.

oyster fritters

serves six

55 g/2 oz plain flour

pinch of salt

pinch of sugar

50 ml/2 fl oz water

2 tsp vegetable oil, plus extra for
deep-frying

1 egg white

36 fresh oysters, shucked
(see page 194)

lemon wedges, to garnish

COOK'S TIP

This is a very light, delicate
batter. It must be used
immediately it is ready and
cannot be made in advance.

1 Sift the flour, salt and sugar into a bowl. Stir in the water and vegetable oil until smooth.

2 Heat the oil for deep-frying in a deep-fat fryer or large saucepan to 180–190°C/350–375°F, or until a cube of bread browns in 30 seconds.

3 Meanwhile, whisk the egg white in a spotlessly clean, greasefree bowl until it forms soft peaks. Gently fold the egg white into the flour mixture until it is fully incorporated.

4 Working in batches, dip the oysters into the batter, then drop them into the hot oil and deep-fry for 3–4 minutes, or until crisp and golden. Remove with a slotted spoon and drain on kitchen paper. Keep warm while you cook the remaining batches, then serve, garnished with lemon wedges.

Meat & Poultry

Most meat and poultry is not as plentiful in Spain as it is in many other countries – pork, including chorizo sausage, and chicken are the main exceptions to the rule and feature heavily in this section. There are also a couple of meatball recipes – meatballs have been a feature of Spanish cooking since at least the thirteenth century.

Many of these dishes work equally well with alternative main ingredients: try slices of fresh turkey, pork or rabbit instead of the chicken on page 223, or replace the chicken livers used on page 224 with lamb's or calf's kidneys.

The Deep-fried Stuffed Dates (see page 214) is one representative of the new-style tapas recipe that has developed in modern Spanish metropolitan cocktail bars.

miniature pork brochettes

makes twelve

450 g/1 lb lean boneless pork
(see Cook's Tip)

3 tbsp Spanish olive oil, plus extra
for oiling (optional)

grated rind and juice of

1 large lemon

2 garlic cloves, crushed

2 tbsp chopped fresh flat-leaf
parsley, plus extra to garnish

1 tbsp ras-el-hanout spice blend
(see Cook's Tip)

salt and pepper

COOK'S TIP

Although usually made with
pork in Spain, these brochettes
are of Arab origin, and would
be made using lamb; both are
delicious. The ras-el-hanout spice
blend, found in delicatessens
and larger supermarkets, consists
of galangal, rosebuds, black
peppercorns, ginger, cardamom,
nigella, cayenne, allspice,
lavender, cinnamon, cassia,
coriander, mace, nutmeg
and cloves!

1 The brochettes are marinated
overnight, so remember to do this
in advance in order that they are ready
when you need them. Cut the pork into
pieces about 2 cm/¾ inch square and
put in a large, shallow, non-metallic
dish that will hold the pieces in a
single layer.

2 To prepare the marinade, place
all the remaining ingredients
in a bowl and mix together. Pour the
marinade over the pork and toss
the meat in it until well coated. Cover
the dish and leave to marinate in the
refrigerator for 8 hours or overnight,
stirring the pork 2–3 times.

3 You can use wooden or metal
skewers to cook the brochettes
and for this recipe you will need about
12 x 15-cm/6-inch skewers. If you are
using wooden ones, soak them in cold
water for 30 minutes prior to using.
This helps to stop them burning and
the food sticking to them during
cooking. Metal skewers simply need
to be greased, and flat ones should
be used in preference to round ones
to prevent the food on them falling off.

4 Preheat the grill, griddle or
barbecue. Thread 3 marinated
pork pieces, leaving a little space
between each piece, onto each
prepared skewer. Cook the brochettes
for 10–15 minutes, or until tender and
lightly charred, turning several times
and basting with the remaining
marinade during cooking. Serve the
pork brochettes piping hot, garnished
with parsley.

lamb skewers with lemon

serves eight

2 garlic cloves, finely chopped

1 Spanish onion, finely chopped

2 tsp finely grated lemon rind

2 tbsp lemon juice

1 tsp fresh thyme leaves

1 tsp ground coriander

1 tsp ground cumin

2 tbsp red wine vinegar

125 ml/4 fl oz olive oil

1 kg/2 lb 4 oz lamb fillet, cut into
2-cm/¾-inch pieces

orange or lemon slices, to garnish

COOK'S TIP

Like quite a few tapas dishes, these little skewers are easy to cook on a barbecue. Place a couple of large sprigs of fresh rosemary on the hot coals to add extra flavour and aroma.

1 Mix the garlic, onion, lemon rind, lemon juice, thyme, coriander, cumin, vinegar and olive oil together in a large, shallow, non-metallic dish, whisking well until thoroughly combined.

2 Thread the pieces of lamb onto 16 wooden skewers and add to the dish, turning well to coat. Cover with clingfilm and leave to marinate in the refrigerator for 2–8 hours, turning occasionally.

3 Preheat the grill to medium. Drain the skewers, reserving the marinade. Cook under the hot grill, turning frequently and brushing with the marinade, for 10 minutes, or until tender and cooked to your liking. Serve immediately, garnished with orange slices.

tiny meatballs with tomato sauce

makes about sixty

olive oil

1 red onion, very finely chopped

500 g/1 lb 2 oz fresh lamb mince

1 large egg, beaten

2 tsp freshly squeezed lemon juice

½ tsp ground cumin

pinch of cayenne pepper, to taste

2 tbsp very finely chopped
    fresh mint

salt and pepper

300 ml/10 fl oz Tomato & Pepper
    Salsa (see page 7), to serve

COOK'S TIP

This is an ideal tapas to serve
at a drinks party because the
meatballs can be made ahead
and both the sauce and
meatballs can be served at
room temperature. If you
freeze the meatballs, allow
3 hours for them to thaw
at room temperature.

1 Heat 1 tablespoon of olive oil in a
frying pan over a medium heat.
Add the onion and fry for 5 minutes,
stirring occasionally, until softened but
not browned.

2 Remove the frying pan from the
heat and leave to cool. Add the
onion to the lamb with the egg, lemon
juice, cumin, cayenne, mint and salt
and pepper to taste in a large bowl.
Use your hands to squeeze all the
ingredients together. Fry a small piece
of the mixture and taste to see if the
seasoning needs adjusting.

3 With wet hands, shape the
mixture into about 60 x 2-cm/
¾-inch balls. Place on a tray and leave
to chill for at least 20 minutes.

4 When ready to cook, heat a small
amount of olive oil in 1 or 2 large
frying pans (the exact amount of oil
will depend on how much fat is in the
lamb). Arrange the meatballs in a
single layer, without overcrowding the
frying pan, and fry over a medium heat
for 5 minutes, or until brown on the
outside but still pink inside. Work in
batches if necessary, keeping the
cooked meatballs warm while you fry
the remainder.

5 Gently reheat the Tomato and
Pepper Salsa and serve with the
meatballs for dipping. The meatballs
are best served warm with reheated
sauce, but they are also enjoyable at
room temperature.

tiny spanish meatballs in almond sauce

serves six–eight

55 g/2 oz white or brown bread,
  crusts removed

3 tbsp water

450 g/1 lb fresh lean pork, beef or
  lamb mince

1 large onion, finely chopped

1 garlic clove, crushed

2 tbsp chopped fresh flat-leaf
  parsley, plus extra to garnish

1 egg, beaten

freshly grated nutmeg

plain flour, for coating

2 tbsp Spanish olive oil

squeeze of lemon juice, to taste

salt and pepper

crusty bread, to serve

ALMOND SAUCE

2 tbsp Spanish olive oil

25 g/1 oz white or brown bread

115 g/4 oz blanched almonds

2 garlic cloves, finely chopped

150 ml/5 fl oz dry white wine

425 ml/15 fl oz vegetable stock

salt and pepper

1 To prepare the meatballs, place the bread in a bowl, add the water and leave to soak for 5 minutes. With your hands, squeeze out the water and return the bread to the dried bowl. Add the pork, onion, garlic, parsley and egg, then season with grated nutmeg and a little salt and pepper. Knead the ingredients well to form a smooth mixture.

2 Spread some flour on a plate. With floured hands, shape the meat mixture into about 30 equal-sized balls, then roll each meatball again in flour until coated.

3 Heat the olive oil in a large, heavy-based frying pan. Add the meatballs, in batches, and fry for 4–5 minutes, or until browned on all sides. Using a slotted spoon, remove the meatballs from the frying pan and reserve.

4 To make the sauce, heat the olive oil in the same frying pan in which the meatballs were fried. Break the bread into pieces, add to the pan with the almonds and fry gently, stirring frequently, until the bread and almonds are golden brown. Add the garlic and fry for a further 30 seconds, then pour in the wine and boil for 1–2 minutes. Season to taste with salt and pepper and leave to cool slightly.

5 Transfer the almond mixture to a food processor. Pour in the vegetable stock and process the mixture until smooth. Return the sauce to the frying pan.

6 Carefully add the fried meatballs to the almond sauce and simmer for 25 minutes, or until the meatballs are tender. Taste the sauce and season with salt and pepper if necessary.

7 Transfer the cooked meatballs and sauce to a warmed serving dish, then add a squeeze of lemon juice to taste and sprinkle with chopped parsley to garnish. Serve piping hot with crusty bread for mopping up the almond sauce.

steak bites with chilli sauce

serves four–six

2 tbsp olive oil

1 onion, chopped

1 tsp paprika

1 garlic clove, finely chopped

1 fresh red chilli, deseeded
    and sliced

400 g/14 oz canned chopped
    tomatoes

2 tbsp dry white wine

1 tbsp tomato purée

1 tbsp sherry vinegar

2 tsp sugar

2 rump steaks, about
    175–225 g/6–8 oz each

2 tsp Tabasco sauce

1 tbsp chopped fresh parsley

salt and pepper

VARIATION

You can also serve bite-sized pieces of pork fillet in this way, but omit the Tabasco sauce and cook for a little longer until the juices run clear when the meat is pierced with the point of a sharp knife.

1 Heat half the olive oil in a heavy-based saucepan. Add the onion and cook over a low heat, stirring occasionally, for 5 minutes, or until softened. Add the paprika, garlic and chilli and cook for a further 2–3 minutes, then stir in the tomatoes with their juices, wine, tomato purée, vinegar and sugar. Simmer gently for 15–20 minutes, or until thickened.

2 Meanwhile, heat a heavy-based frying pan or griddle pan over a high heat and brush with the remaining olive oil. Season the steaks to taste with pepper and rub with the Tabasco, then add to the pan. Cook for 1–1½ minutes on each side, or until browned. Reduce the heat and cook, turning once, for 3 minutes for rare, 4–5 minutes for medium or 5–7 minutes for well done. Remove from the heat and keep warm.

3 Transfer the sauce to a food processor or blender and process until fairly smooth. Transfer to a serving bowl, season to taste with salt and pepper and stir in the parsley.

4 Transfer the steaks to a chopping board and cut into bite-sized pieces. Impale on wooden cocktail sticks, place on serving plates and serve immediately with the sauce.

mixed tapas platter with beef

serves eight–ten

200 g/7 oz small waxy potatoes,
  unpeeled
5 tbsp olive oil
2 sirloin steaks, about
  225 g/8 oz each
1 fresh red chilli, deseeded and
  finely chopped (optional)
350 g/12 oz Queso del Montsec or
  other goat's cheese, sliced
175 g/6 oz mixed salad leaves
2 tbsp black olives
2 tbsp green olives
55 g/2 oz canned anchovies in oil,
  drained and halved lengthways
1 tbsp capers, drained and rinsed
salt and pepper

COOK'S TIP

Choose a colourful selection of
salad leaves for an attractive
appearance and combination of
flavours – oak leaf lettuce,
radicchio, frisée and rocket or
watercress, for example. You can
add extra salad ingredients, such
as cherry tomatoes, if you like.

1 Cook the potatoes in a saucepan
of lightly salted boiling water for
15–20 minutes, or until just tender.
Drain and leave to cool slightly.

2 Heat a heavy-based frying pan or
griddle pan over a high heat and
brush with 1 tablespoon of the olive
oil. Season the steaks to taste with
pepper and add to the pan. Cook for
1–1½ minutes on each side, or until
browned. Reduce the heat to medium
and cook for 1½ minutes on each side.
Remove and rest for 10–15 minutes.

3 Heat 2 tablespoons of the
remaining oil in a frying pan. Add
the chilli, if using, and the potatoes
and cook, turning frequently, for
10 minutes, or until crisp and golden.

4 Thinly slice the steaks and
arrange the slices alternately with
the cheese slices along the sides of a
serving platter. Mix the salad leaves,
olives, anchovies and capers together,
then arrange along the centre of the
platter. Drizzle with the remaining oil,
then top with the potatoes. Serve
warm or at room temperature.

beef skewers with orange & garlic

serves six–eight

3 tbsp white wine

2 tbsp olive oil

3 garlic cloves, finely chopped

juice of 1 orange

450 g/1 lb rump steak, cubed

450 g/1 lb baby onions, halved

2 orange peppers, deseeded and
   cut into squares

225 g/8 oz cherry tomatoes, halved

salt and pepper

COOK'S TIP

If you are using wooden or
bamboo skewers, soak them
in cold water for 30 minutes
before use to prevent them
burning under the grill.

1 Mix the wine, olive oil, garlic
and orange juice together in a
shallow, non-metallic dish. Add the
cubes of steak, season to taste with
salt and pepper and toss to coat. Cover
with clingfilm and leave to marinate in
the refrigerator for 2–8 hours.

2 Preheat the grill to high. Drain
the steak, reserving the marinade.
Thread the steak, onions, peppers
and tomatoes alternately onto several
small skewers.

3 Cook under the hot grill,
turning and brushing frequently
with the marinade, for 10 minutes,
or until cooked through. Transfer
to warmed serving plates and serve
immediately.

serrano ham with rocket

serves six

140 g/5 oz rocket, separated
  into leaves

4½ tbsp olive oil

1½ tbsp orange juice

280 g/10 oz thinly sliced
  serrano ham

salt and pepper

1 Place the rocket in a bowl and
pour in the olive oil and orange
juice. Season to taste with salt and
pepper and toss well.

2 Arrange the slices of ham on
individual serving plates, folding
it into attractive shapes. Divide the
rocket between the plates and
serve immediately.

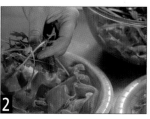

COOK'S TIP

Jamón de Jabugo from the
Huelva region is the ideal ham
for this tapa, as its intrinsic
sweetness contrasts beautifully
with the peppery flavour
of rocket.

cheese & ham pastries

serves six

6 slices serrano ham

Tabasco sauce, for brushing

200 g/7 oz Queso Majorero,
    Manchego or goat's cheese

6 sheets filo pastry, about
    46 x 28 cm/18 x 11 inches

3–4 tbsp olive oil

COOK'S TIP
Filo is not, of course, a
typically Spanish ingredient,
although ouarka, a similar
pastry from North Africa, is
found in southern Spain.

1 Preheat the oven to 200°C/400°F/
Gas Mark 6. Spread out the ham
and brush with Tabasco to taste. Cut
the cheese into 6 slices. Wrap a slice of
cheese in each slice of ham.

2 Working on one sheet of pastry at
a time and keeping the others
covered with a clean, damp tea towel,
brush with a little olive oil, then fold in
half. Place 1 ham-wrapped slice of
cheese in the centre, brush the pastry
with oil again and fold it over to
enclose it completely. Place on a
baking sheet, seam-side down, and
brush the top with a little oil. Repeat
with the remaining sheets of filo and
ham-wrapped cheese.

3 Bake in the preheated oven for
15 minutes, or until golden
brown and crisp. Serve immediately or
leave to cool slightly and serve warm.

ham & almond fritters

serves four–six

70 g/2½ oz plain flour

150 ml/5 fl oz water

55 g/2 oz butter

2 eggs

55 g/2 oz flaked almonds

115 g/4 oz ham, chopped

vegetable oil, for deep-frying

salt and pepper

1 Sift the flour with a pinch of salt and pepper onto a sheet of greaseproof paper. Bring the water to the boil in a heavy-based saucepan. Add the butter and as soon as it has melted remove the saucepan from the heat. Tip in the flour and beat well with a wooden spoon until the mixture comes away from the side of the saucepan.

2 Beat in the eggs, one at a time, and continue to beat until the mixture is glossy. Fold in the flaked almonds and ham and leave the mixture to cool.

3 Heat the vegetable oil in a deep-fat fryer or large saucepan to 180–190°C/350–375°F, or until a cube of bread browns in 30 seconds.

4 Working in batches, drop heaped tablespoonfuls of the mixture into the hot oil and deep-fry for 3–4 minutes, or until crisp and golden. Remove with a slotted spoon and drain on kitchen paper. Serve the fritters hot.

VARIATION

You could also make these fritters with diced chorizo sausage instead of ham. Make sure that you buy ready-to-eat chorizo rather than the cooking sausage, as the fritters will puff up before the raw sausage is cooked.

chorizo & mushroom kebabs

makes twenty-five

2 tbsp olive oil

25 pieces chorizo sausage, each
about 1-cm/½-inch square
(about 100 g/3½ oz)

25 button mushrooms, wiped and
stalks removed

1 green pepper, grilled, peeled
(see Cook's Tip) and cut into
5 squares

COOK'S TIP

To peel peppers, halve them
lengthways, stem on, which
makes removal of the core and
seeds simpler. Grill, skin-sides up,
5–7.5 cm/2–3 inches from the
heat, until charred. Remove from
the heat and place in a polythene
bag for 15 minutes, then rub or
peel off the skins. Remove any
cores and seeds. Alternatively,
the peppers can be charred over
a flame. Grilled and peeled
peppers can be kept for up to
5 days in the refrigerator,
covered with olive oil.

1 Heat the olive oil in a frying pan
over a medium heat. Add the
chorizo and fry for 20 seconds, stirring.

2 Add the mushrooms and continue
frying for a further 1–2 minutes
until the mushrooms begin to brown
and absorb the fat in the frying pan.

3 Thread a green pepper square, a
piece of chorizo and a mushroom
on to a wooden cocktail stick. Continue
until all the ingredients are used. Serve
hot or at room temperature.

deep-fried stuffed dates

serves six

1 ready-to-eat chorizo sausage

12 fresh dates

6 bacon rashers, rinds removed

25 g/1 oz plain flour, for dusting

1 egg, lightly beaten

55 g/2 oz fresh white breadcrumbs

vegetable oil, for deep-frying

VARIATION

You can also stuff fresh dates with diced cheese before coating with egg and breadcrumbs and deep-frying.

1 Remove the outer casing from the chorizo and cut the sausage into 3 slices. Cut each slice into quarters.

2 Slit the sides of the dates with a sharp knife and remove and discard the stones. Insert a piece of chorizo into each cavity. Stretch the bacon rashers with the back of a knife, then cut each rasher in half across the centre. Wrap a piece of bacon around each date.

3 Place the flour, egg and breadcrumbs in separate shallow dishes. Coat the dates in the flour, then in the egg, then in the breadcrumbs. Meanwhile, heat the vegetable oil in a deep-fat fryer or large saucepan to 180–190°C/350–375°F, or until a cube of bread browns in 30 seconds.

4 Deep-fry the stuffed dates, in batches if necessary, turning them occasionally, for 3–4 minutes, or until golden brown all over. Remove with a slotted spoon and drain on kitchen paper. Serve hot.

chorizo empanadillas

makes twelve

125 g/4½ oz chorizo sausage,
  outer casing removed
250 g/9 oz ready-made puff pastry,
  thawed if frozen
plain flour, for dusting
beaten egg, to glaze
TO GARNISH
paprika
fresh basil sprigs

1 Preheat the oven to 200°C/
400°F/Gas Mark 6. Cut the
chorizo into small dice measuring
about 1 cm/½ inch square. Thinly roll
out the puff pastry on a lightly floured
work surface. Using a plain, round
8-cm/3¼-inch cutter, cut into rounds.
Gently pile the trimmings together, roll
out again, then cut out further rounds
to produce 12 in total.

2 Place about 1 teaspoon of the
chopped chorizo onto each of
the pastry rounds. Dampen the edges
of the pastry with a little water,
then fold one half over the other half
to completely cover the chorizo. Seal
the edges together with your fingers.
Using the tines of a fork, press against
the edges to give a decorative finish
and seal them further. With the point
of a sharp knife, make a small slit in
the side of each pastry. You can store
the pastries in the refrigerator at this
stage until you are ready to bake them.

3 Place the pastries onto dampened
baking trays and brush each with
a little beaten egg to glaze. Bake in the
preheated oven for 10–15 minutes,
or until golden brown and puffed.
Using a small sieve, lightly dust the
top of each empanadilla with a little
paprika and garnish with herb sprigs.
Serve hot or warm.

chorizo & quail's eggs

makes twelve

12 slices French bread, sliced on
    the diagonal, about 5 mm/
    ¼ inch thick

40 g/1½ oz cured, ready-to-eat
    chorizo, cut into 12 thin slices

olive oil

12 quail's eggs

mild paprika

salt and pepper

fresh flat-leaf parsley, to garnish

COOK'S TIP

Despite their delicate
appearance, quail's eggs can
be difficult to crack because of
a relatively thick membrane
under the shell. It is useful to
have a pair of scissors handy
to cut through the membrane
as you break the eggs into
the frying pan.

1 Preheat the grill to high. Arrange the slices of bread on a baking sheet and grill until golden brown on both sides.

2 Cut or fold the chorizo slices to fit on the toasts, then reserve.

3 Heat a thin layer of olive oil in a large frying pan over a medium heat until a cube of bread sizzles — about 40 seconds. Break the eggs into the frying pan and fry, spooning the fat over the yolks, until the whites are set and the yolks are cooked to your liking.

4 Remove the fried eggs from the frying pan and drain on kitchen paper. Immediately transfer to the chorizo-topped toasts and dust with paprika. Season to taste with salt and pepper, garnish with parsley and serve immediately.

chorizo in red wine

serves six

200 g/7 oz chorizo sausage

200 ml/7 fl oz Spanish red wine

2 tbsp brandy (optional)

fresh flat-leaf parsley sprigs,
   to garnish

crusty bread, to serve

1 Before you begin, bear in mind that this dish is best if prepared the day before you are planning to serve it. Using a fork, prick the chorizo in 3 or 4 places and pour wine over. Place the chorizo and wine in a large saucepan. Bring the wine to the boil, then reduce the heat, cover and simmer gently for 15–20 minutes. Transfer the chorizo and wine to a bowl or dish, cover and leave the sausage to marinate in the wine for 8 hours or overnight.

2 The next day, remove the chorizo from the bowl or dish and reserve the wine. Remove the outer casing from the chorizo and cut the sausage into 5-mm/¼-inch slices. Place the slices in a large, heavy-based frying pan or flameproof serving dish.

3 If you are adding the brandy, pour it into a small saucepan and heat gently. Pour the brandy over the chorizo slices, stand well back and set alight. When the flames have died down, shake the saucepan gently, add the reserved wine to the saucepan and cook over a high heat until almost all of the wine has evaporated.

4 Serve the chorizo in red wine piping hot, in the dish in which it was cooked, sprinkled with parsley to garnish. Accompany with chunks or slices of bread to mop up the juices and provide wooden cocktail sticks to spear the pieces of chorizo.

fried chorizo with herbs

serves six–eight

700 g/1 lb 9 oz chorizo cooking
sausage

2 tbsp olive oil

2 garlic cloves, finely chopped

4 tbsp chopped mixed fresh herbs

COOK'S TIP

Chorizo may be mild or hot and it
is available both smoked and
unsmoked. All types of cooking
sausage are suitable for this dish.

1 Using a sharp knife, cut the
chorizo into 5-mm/¼-inch thick
slices. Heat a large, heavy-based frying
pan. Add the chorizo slices, without
any additional fat, and cook over a
medium heat, stirring frequently, for
5 minutes, or until crisp and browned.

2 Remove the chorizo slices with a
spatula or slotted spoon and
drain well on kitchen paper. Drain the
fat from the frying pan and wipe out
with a pad of kitchen paper.

3 Heat the olive oil in the frying pan
over a medium–low heat. Add
the chorizo slices, garlic and herbs and
cook, stirring occasionally, until heated
through. Serve immediately.

chickpeas & chorizo

serves four–six

250 g/9 oz chorizo sausage in
　　1 piece, outer casing removed

4 tbsp olive oil

1 onion, finely chopped

1 large garlic clove, crushed

400 g/14 oz canned chickpeas,
　　drained and rinsed

6 pimientos del piquillo
　　(see page 160), drained,
　　patted dry and sliced

1 tbsp sherry vinegar, or to taste

salt and pepper

finely chopped fresh parsley,
　　to garnish

crusty bread slices, to serve

1 Cut the chorizo into 1-cm/½-inch dice. Heat the oil in a large, heavy-based frying pan over a medium heat. Add the onion and garlic and fry, stirring occasionally, until the onion is softened but not browned. Stir in the chorizo and fry until heated through.

2 Tip the mixture into a bowl and stir in the chickpeas and pimientos. Splash with sherry vinegar and season to taste with salt and pepper. Serve hot or at room temperature, generously sprinkled with parsley, with plenty of crusty bread.

chicken in lemon & garlic

serves six–eight

4 large skinless, boneless
   chicken breasts

5 tbsp Spanish olive oil

1 onion, finely chopped

6 garlic cloves, finely chopped

grated rind of 1 lemon, finely pared
   rind of 1 lemon and juice of
   both lemons

4 tbsp chopped fresh flat-leaf
   parsley, plus extra to garnish

salt and pepper

TO SERVE

lemon wedges

crusty bread

1 Using a sharp knife, slice the chicken breasts widthways into very thin slices. Heat the olive oil in a large, heavy-based frying pan. Add the onion and fry for 5 minutes, or until softened but not browned. Add the garlic and fry for a further 30 seconds.

2 Add the sliced chicken to the frying pan and fry gently for 5–10 minutes, stirring occasionally, until all the ingredients are lightly browned and the chicken is tender.

3 Add the grated lemon rind and the lemon juice and let it bubble. At the same time, deglaze the pan by scraping and stirring all the bits on the base of the pan into the juices with a wooden spoon. Remove the pan from the heat, stir in the parsley and season to taste with salt and pepper.

4 Transfer the chicken in lemon and garlic, piping hot, to a warmed serving dish. Sprinkle with the pared lemon rind, garnish with parsley sprigs and serve with lemon wedges for squeezing over the chicken, accompanied by chunks or slices of crusty bread for mopping up the lemon and garlic juices.

chicken livers in sherry sauce

serves six

450 g/1 lb chicken livers

2 tbsp Spanish olive oil

1 small onion, finely chopped

2 garlic cloves, finely chopped

100 ml/3½ fl oz dry Spanish sherry

2 tbsp chopped fresh flat-leaf
    parsley, plus extra sprigs,
    to garnish

salt and pepper

crusty bread or toast, to serve

1 If necessary, trim the chicken livers, cutting away any ducts and gristle, then cut them into small, bite-sized pieces. Heat the olive oil in a large, heavy-based frying pan. Add the onion and fry for 5 minutes, or until softened but not browned. Add the garlic and fry for a further 30 seconds.

2 Add the chicken livers to the pan and fry for 2–3 minutes, stirring constantly, until they are firm and have changed colour on the outside but are still pink and soft in the centre. Using a slotted spoon, lift the chicken livers from the pan, transfer them to a large, warmed serving dish or several smaller ones and keep warm.

3 Add the sherry to the frying pan, increase the heat and let it bubble for 3–4 minutes to evaporate the alcohol and reduce slightly. At the same time, deglaze the pan by scraping and stirring all the bits on the base of the pan into the sauce with a wooden spoon. Season the sauce to taste with salt and pepper.

4 Pour the sherry sauce over the chicken livers and sprinkle over the parsley. Garnish with parsley sprigs and serve piping hot with chunks or slices of crusty bread or toast to mop up the sauce.

spicy chicken livers

serves four–six

115 g/4 oz plain flour

½ tsp ground cumin

½ tsp ground coriander

½ tsp paprika

¼ tsp freshly grated nutmeg

350 g/12 oz chicken livers

6 tbsp olive oil

salt and pepper

fresh mint sprigs, to garnish

COOK'S TIP

Frozen chicken livers are widely available and very inexpensive. They are usually sold packed into plastic tubs. Turn them out onto a dish and thaw completely before using.

1 Sift the flour onto a large, shallow plate and stir in the cumin, coriander, paprika and nutmeg. Season to taste with salt and pepper.

2 Trim the chicken livers and pat dry with kitchen paper. Cut the livers in halves or quarters. Toss in the seasoned flour, a few pieces at a time, shaking off any excess.

3 Heat the olive oil in a large, heavy-based frying pan. Cook the livers, in batches, over a high heat, stirring frequently, for 3–5 minutes, or until crisp on the outside but still tender in the centre. Serve impaled on wooden cocktail sticks and garnished with mint sprigs.

chicken wings with tomato dressing

serves six–eight

175 ml/6 fl oz olive oil

3 garlic cloves, finely chopped

1 tsp ground cumin

1 kg/1 lb 4 oz chicken wings

2 tomatoes, peeled, deseeded (see
page 167) and diced

5 tbsp white wine vinegar

1 tbsp shredded fresh basil leaves

VARIATION

You can also serve chicken
drumsticks in this way, but they
will need a longer cooking time
in the oven – about 25–30
minutes. Test in the same way as
the chicken wings to check if
they are thoroughly cooked.

1 Preheat the oven to 180°C/
350°F/Gas Mark 4. Mix
1 tablespoon of the oil, the garlic and
cumin together in a shallow dish. Cut
off and discard the tips of the chicken
wings and add the wings to the spice
mixture, turning to coat. Cover with
clingfilm and leave to marinate in a
cool place for 15 minutes.

2 Heat 3 tablespoons of the
remaining oil in a large, heavy-
based frying pan. Add the chicken
wings, in batches, and cook, turning
frequently, until golden brown. Transfer
to a roasting tin.

3 Roast the chicken wings for
10–15 minutes, or until tender
and the juices run clear when the point
of a sharp knife is inserted into the
thickest part of the meat.

4 Meanwhile, mix the remaining
olive oil, the tomatoes, vinegar
and basil together in a bowl.

5 Using tongs, transfer the chicken
wings to a non-metallic dish.
Pour the dressing over them, turning
to coat. Cover with clingfilm, leave to
cool, then chill for 4 hours. Remove
from the refrigerator 30–60 minutes
before serving to return to them to
room temperature.

chicken rolls with olives

serves six–eight

115 g/4 oz black olives in oil, drained

140 g/5 oz butter, softened

4 tbsp chopped fresh parsley

4 skinless, boneless chicken breasts

2 tbsp oil from the olive jar

1 Preheat the oven to 200°C/ 400°F/Gas Mark 6. Stone and chop the olives. Mix half the olives, the butter and parsley together in a bowl.

2 Place the chicken breasts between 2 sheets of clingfilm and beat gently with a meat mallet or the side of rolling pin.

3 Spread the olive and herb butter over one side of each flattened chicken breast and roll up. Secure with a wooden cocktail stick or tie with clean string if necessary.

VARIATION

You can substitute chilli oil for the oil from the olive jar. This is available commercially or you can make your own by infusing 2–3 fresh red bird's-eye chillies in 600 ml/1 pint of olive oil in a sterilized screw-top jar for about 3 weeks. Strain into a clean jar or bottle before using.

4 Place the chicken rolls in an ovenproof dish. Drizzle over the oil from the olive jar and bake in the preheated oven for 45–55 minutes, or until tender and the juices run clear when the chicken is pierced with the point of a sharp knife.

5 Transfer the chicken rolls to a chopping board and discard the cocktail sticks or string. Using a sharp knife, cut into slices, then transfer to warmed serving plates and serve.

crispy chicken & ham croquettes

makes eight

4 tbsp olive oil or 55 g/2 oz butter

4 tbsp plain flour

200 ml/7 fl oz milk

115 g/4 oz cooked chicken, minced

55 g/2 oz serrano or cooked ham,
   very finely chopped

1 tbsp chopped fresh flat-leaf
   parsley, plus extra sprigs
   to garnish

small pinch of freshly grated nutmeg

1 egg, beaten

55 g/2 oz day-old white
   breadcrumbs

sunflower oil, for deep-frying

salt and pepper

Aïoli (see page 12), to serve

1 Heat the olive oil or butter in a saucepan. Stir in the flour to form a paste and cook gently for 1 minute, stirring constantly. Remove the saucepan from the heat and gradually stir in the milk until smooth. Return to the heat and slowly bring to the boil, stirring constantly, until the mixture boils and begins to thicken.

2 Remove the saucepan from the heat, add the minced chicken and beat until the mixture is smooth. Add the chopped ham, parsley and nutmeg and mix well. Season the mixture to taste with salt and pepper. Spread the chicken mixture in a dish and leave for 30 minutes until cool, then cover and leave to chill for 2–3 hours or overnight. Don't be tempted to miss out this stage, as chilling the croquettes helps to stop them falling apart when they are cooked.

3 When the chicken mixture has chilled, pour the beaten egg onto a plate and spread the breadcrumbs out on a separate plate. Divide the chicken mixture into 8 equal-sized portions. With dampened hands, form each portion into a cylindrical shape. Dip the croquettes, one at a time, in the beaten egg, then roll in the breadcrumbs to coat them. Place on a plate

4 To cook, heat the sunflower oil in a deep-fat fryer to 180–190°C/ 350–375°F, or until a cube of bread browns in 30 seconds. Add the croquettes, in batches to prevent the temperature of the oil dropping, and deep-fry for 5–10 minutes, or until golden brown and crispy. Remove with a slotted spoon and drain well on kitchen paper.

5 Serve the chicken and ham croquettes piping hot, garnished with parsley sprigs and accompanied by a bowl of Aïoli for dipping.

Bread & Pizzas

Considering the evolution of tapas from the original slices of bread, topped with other ingredients, to a cosmopolitan and varied cuisine enjoyed the world over, it seems fitting to end this book with a selection of bread-based recipes as well as dishes that share a lineage with the cooking of other nations. The Prawn & Haricot Toasties (see page 248) are actually a local pizza-style dish. Variations include many toppings found on pizzas, such as anchovies, peppers and ham, but seldom cheese. The Chorizo Pizza (see page 252) is, however, an Italian-style pizza with a Spanish twist.

flat bread with vegetables & clams

serves four–six

2 tbsp extra virgin olive oil

4 large garlic cloves, crushed

2 large onions, thinly sliced

10 pimientos del piquillo
(see page 160), drained, patted
dry and thinly sliced

250 g/9 oz shelled baby clams in
brine (weight in jar), drained
and rinsed

salt and pepper

DOUGH

400 g/14 oz strong white flour,
plus extra for dusting

1 sachet easy-blend dried yeast

1 tsp salt

½ tsp sugar

1 tbsp olive oil, plus extra for oiling

1 tbsp dry white wine

225 ml/8 fl oz warm water

1 To make the dough, stir the flour, yeast, salt and sugar together in a bowl, making a well in the centre. Add the olive oil and wine to the water, then pour 175 ml/6 fl oz of the liquid into the well. Gradually mix in the flour from the sides, adding the remaining liquid if necessary, until a soft dough forms.

2 Turn out the dough onto a lightly floured surface and knead until smooth. Shape the dough into a ball. Wash the bowl and rub the inside with olive oil. Return the dough to the bowl and roll it around so that it is lightly coated in oil. Cover the bowl tightly with clingfilm and leave in a warm place until the dough doubles in size.

3 Heat the olive oil in a large, heavy-based frying pan over a medium heat. Reduce the heat and add the garlic and onions and fry slowly, stirring frequently, for 25 minutes, or until the onions are golden brown but not burned.

4 Preheat the oven to 230°C/450°F/ Gas Mark 8. Transfer the onions to a bowl and leave to cool. Add the pepper strips and clams to the bowl and stir together. Reserve.

5 Knock back the dough and knead quickly on a lightly floured work surface. Cover it with the upturned bowl and leave for 10 minutes, which will make it easier to roll out.

6 Heavily flour a 32 x 32-cm/ 12¾ x 12¾-inch shallow baking tray. Roll out the dough to make a 34-cm/13½-inch square and transfer it to the baking tray, rolling the edges to form a thin rim. Prick the base all over with a fork.

7 Spread the topping evenly over the dough and season to taste with salt and pepper. Bake in the preheated oven for 25 minutes, or until the rim is golden brown and the onions tips are slightly tinged. Transfer to a wire rack to cool completely. Cut into 12–16 slices.

salads on bread

each salad quantity makes 12–14 open sandwiches

POTATO SALAD

200 g/7 oz new potatoes, scrubbed
  and boiled

½ tbsp white wine vinegar

3–4 tbsp mayonnaise

2 hard-boiled eggs, shelled and
  finely chopped

2 spring onions, white and green
  parts finely chopped

1 large French bread

salt and pepper

12–14 black olives, stoned and
  sliced, to garnish

TUNA SALAD

200 g/7 oz canned tuna in olive
  oil, drained

4 tbsp mayonnaise

2 hard-boiled eggs, shelled and
  finely chopped

1 tomato, grilled and peeled,
  deseeded (see page 167) and
  very finely chopped

2 tsp grated lemon rind, or to taste

cayenne pepper, to taste

1 large French bread

salt and pepper

12–14 anchovy fillets in oil,
  drained, to garnish

1 To make the potato salad, peel the potatoes as soon as they are cool enough to handle, then cut into 5-mm/¼-inch dice. Toss with the vinegar and season to taste with salt and pepper. Leave to cool completely. Stir in the mayonnaise, then fold in the eggs and spring onions. Taste and adjust the seasoning. Cut the bread on a slight diagonal, 5 mm/¼ inch thick, into 24–28 slices. Mound the salad on the bread, then top with olive slices.

2 To make the tuna salad, flake the tuna into a bowl. Stir in the mayonnaise, then fold in the eggs, tomato, lemon rind and cayenne. Taste and adjust the seasoning. Cut the bread on a slight diagonal, 5 mm/ ¼ inch thick, into 24–28 slices. Mound the salad on the bread, then top with anchovy fillets.

spicy fried bread & chorizo

serves six–eight

200 g/7 oz chorizo sausage,
  outer casing removed
4 thick slices 2-day-old
  country bread
Spanish olive oil, for shallow-frying
3 garlic cloves, finely chopped
2 tbsp chopped fresh
  flat-leaf parsley
paprika, to garnish

COOK'S TIP

Choose a soft chorizo sausage for this recipe because, although it will not have been cured for a long period, the soft varieties usually contain a high proportion of fat, which makes them very good for cooking. As an alternative to chorizo, you could use thickly cut serrano ham or even garlic sausage.

1 Cut the chorizo into 1-cm/½-inch thick slices and cut the bread, with its crusts still on, into 1-cm/½-inch cubes. Add enough olive oil to a large, heavy-based frying pan so that it generously covers the base. Heat the oil, add the garlic and fry for 30 seconds–1 minute, or until lightly browned.

2 Add the bread cubes to the pan and fry, stirring constantly, until golden brown and crisp. Add the chorizo slices and fry for 1–2 minutes, or until hot. Using a slotted spoon, remove the bread cubes and chorizo from the frying pan and drain well on kitchen paper.

3 Turn the fried bread and chorizo into a warmed serving bowl, add the chopped parsley and toss together. Garnish the dish with a sprinkling of paprika and serve warm. Accompany with wooden cocktail sticks so that a piece of sausage and a cube of bread can be speared together for eating.

crusty bread with beans & chorizo

serves six

3 garlic cloves

4 tbsp olive oil

1 Spanish onion, finely chopped

140 g/5 oz chorizo cooking
    sausage, sliced

800 g/1 lb 12 oz canned haricot
    beans, drained and rinsed

6 thick slices country bread

4 tomatoes, chopped

salt and pepper

fresh parsley sprigs, to garnish

1 Thinly slice 2 of the garlic cloves. Heat half the olive oil in a large, heavy-based frying pan. Add the onion and sliced garlic and cook over a low heat, stirring occasionally, for 5 minutes, or until softened. Meanwhile, cut the chorizo slices in half.

VARIATION

You can use other beans for this dish – try flageolets, cannellini or even ful medames for a hint of North African cuisine.

2 Stir the chorizo into the frying pan and cook for a further 2 minutes, then add the beans. Season to taste with salt and pepper.

3 Griddle or toast the bread on both sides. Meanwhile, stir the tomatoes into the frying pan.

4 Halve the remaining garlic clove and rub the cut sides over the toast, then drizzle the toast with the remaining oil.

5 Place the griddled bread on individual serving plates and divide the bean and chorizo mixture between the slices. Serve immediately, garnished with parsley sprigs.

little breads with bean purée

serves four

225 g/8 oz dried haricot beans

½ onion, finely chopped

2 tbsp olive oil

2 tbsp chopped fresh mint

4 thick slices country bread

salt and pepper

COOK'S TIP

Cover the bowl of bean purée with clingfilm and store in the refrigerator until required. Return to room temperature before serving.

1 Place the beans in a bowl and add enough cold water to cover. Leave to soak for 4 hours, or preferably overnight, then drain.

2 Place the beans in a saucepan and add the onion. Pour in enough water to cover and bring to the boil. Cook for 1½ hours, or until tender, then drain well and leave to cool slightly.

3 Toast the bread on both sides. Transfer the beans to a food processor or blender and process to a purée. Scrape into a serving bowl and stir in the olive oil and mint. Season to taste with salt and pepper. Divide the purée between the slices of toast and serve at room temperature.

salt cod on garlic toasts

serves six

200 g/7 oz dried salt cod

5 garlic cloves

225 ml/8 fl oz olive oil

225 ml/8 fl oz double cream

6 thick slices country bread

pepper

1 Soak the dried salt cod in cold water for 48 hours, changing the water 3 times a day. Drain well, then cut into chunks and place in a large, shallow frying pan. Pour in enough cold water to cover and bring to simmering point. Poach for 8–10 minutes, or until tender. Drain well and leave until cool enough to handle.

2 Finely chop 4 of the garlic cloves. Halve the remaining clove and reserve until required.

3 Remove and discard the skin from the fish. Roughly chop the flesh and place in a food processor or blender.

4 Pour the olive oil into a saucepan and add the chopped garlic. Bring to simmering point over a low heat. Pour the cream into a separate saucepan and bring to simmering point over a low heat. Remove both saucepans from the heat.

5 Process the fish briefly. With the motor still running, add a little of the garlic oil and process. With the motor still running, add a little cream and process. Continue in this way until all the garlic oil and cream have been incorporated. Scrape the mixture into a serving bowl and season to taste with pepper.

6 Toast the bread on both sides, then rub each slice with the cut sides of the reserved garlic. Pile the fish mixture onto the toasts and serve.

tomato bread

serves four

sliced bread or French bread

tomatoes

garlic (optional)

olive oil (optional)

1 At its simplest, slices of bread are rubbed with half a fresh juicy tomato. If the bread is soft, you can toast it first. Other options are to flavour it with garlic, or drizzle olive oil over the top.

tomato toasts with three toppings

serves four–six

12 thick slices country bread

12 tomatoes, peeled, deseeded
(see page 167) and diced

8 garlic cloves, finely chopped

about 350 ml/12 fl oz olive oil

salt and pepper

HAM & CAPER TOPPING

2 slices ham, cut into thin strips

8 capers, drained and rinsed

CHORIZO & CHEESE TOPPING

8 slices ready-to eat
chorizo sausage

55 g/2 oz Manchego or Cheddar
cheese, sliced

2 pimiento-stuffed olives, halved

ANCHOVY & OLIVE TOPPING

12 canned anchovy fillets in
oil, drained

4 anchovy-stuffed green olives

COOK'S TIP
You can make smaller toasts by
using French bread or you can
stamp out rounds from
wholemeal or Granary bread
with a biscuit cutter.

---

1 Toast the bread on both sides.
Meanwhile, place the tomatoes in
a bowl and break up with a fork, then
mix in the garlic. Spread the tomato
mixture evenly over the toast, season
to taste with salt and pepper and
drizzle with the olive oil.

2 For the ham and caper topping,
arrange the strips of ham in an 'S'
shape across 4 of the toasts and place
a caper in the curves of each letter 'S'.

3 For the chorizo and cheese
topping, place 2 slices of chorizo
on each of 4 of the remaining toasts
and top with the cheese. Garnish with
an olive half.

4 For the anchovy and olive
topping, curl 3 anchovy fillets into
circles, place on the remaining 4 toasts
and put an olive in the centre of each.

grilled tomatoes on bread

serves four

3 tbsp olive oil

6 tomatoes, thickly sliced

4 thick slices country bread

1 garlic clove, halved

4 tsp sherry vinegar

salt and pepper

VARIATION

For a garnish, add a few shavings of Manchego, Queso Iberico or other hard cheese.

1 Heat a ridged griddle pan and brush with 1 tablespoon of the olive oil. Add the tomato slices and cook over a high heat for 2 minutes on each side, or until softened and beginning to char.

2 Meanwhile, toast the bread on both sides, then rub each slice with the cut sides of the garlic.

3 Divide the tomato slices between the slices of toast and drizzle with the remaining oil and the vinegar. Season to taste with salt and pepper and serve.

asparagus rolls

serves eight

115 g/4 oz butter, softened,
   plus extra for greasing
8 asparagus spears, trimmed
8 slices white bread, crusts removed
1 tbsp chopped fresh parsley
finely grated rind of 1 orange
salt and pepper

1 Preheat the oven to 190°C/
375°F/Gas Mark 5 and lightly
grease a baking sheet. If woody,
peel the asparagus stems, then tie
the spears loosely together with
clean kitchen string. Blanch in a tall
saucepan of boiling water for
3–5 minutes. Drain and refresh under
cold running water. Drain again and
pat dry with kitchen paper.

2 Lightly flatten the slices of bread
with a rolling pin. Mix 70 g/2½ oz
of the butter, the parsley and orange
rind together in a bowl and season to
taste with salt and pepper. Spread the
flavoured butter over the bread slices.

3 Place an asparagus spear near
one side of a bread slice and
roll up. Repeat with the remaining
asparagus spears and bread. Place
the asparagus rolls, seam-side down,
on the baking sheet.

4 Melt the remaining butter in a
small saucepan, then brush it
over the asparagus rolls. Bake in the
preheated oven for 15 minutes, or until
crisp and golden brown. Leave to cool
slightly, then serve warm.

COOK'S TIP

If fresh asparagus is not
available, use frozen. Thaw
completely before using and omit
Step 1. Canned asparagus tends
to be too soggy for this tapa.

anchovy rolls

serves four

butter, for greasing and spreading

8 salted anchovies

50 ml/2 fl oz milk

4 slices white bread, crusts removed

1 tbsp Dijon mustard

2 tbsp grated Manchego or
   Cheddar cheese

COOK'S TIP

Whole anchovies packed in salt
are becoming increasingly
available. They are very salty and
always need soaking. However,
if you cannot find them, use
12 drained, canned anchovy
fillets in oil. These are also quite
salty, but it is a matter of taste
whether to soak them or not.

1 Preheat the oven to 220°C/
425°F/Gas Mark 7. Lightly grease
a baking sheet. Place the anchovies
in a small, shallow dish and pour
over the milk. Leave to soak for
10–15 minutes. Drain, discarding the
milk, and pat dry with kitchen paper.

2 Spread each bread slice with
butter and then with mustard.
Sprinkle with the grated cheese. Divide
the anchovy between the bread slices
and roll up.

3 Place on the baking sheet,
seam-side down, and bake in
the preheated oven for 6–7 minutes.
Leave to cool slightly, then serve.

olive & red pepper bread

serves four–six

2 red peppers, halved and
deseeded

3 garlic cloves

2 tsp capers, drained, rinsed
and halved

4 tbsp chopped fresh parsley

1 tbsp lemon juice

1 tsp ground cumin

2 tsp sugar

55 g/2 oz black olives, stoned
and chopped

1 French bread

2 tbsp olive oil

VARIATION

For olive and aubergine bread,
replace the peppers with 1 large
or 2 medium aubergines.
Slash the skins and bake
in a preheated oven at
200°C/400°F/Gas Mark 6 for
30 minutes, or until softened.
Leave to cool slightly, then peel
off the skin and place the flesh in
a food processor or blender.
Proceed from Step 2.

1 Preheat the grill to high. Place the pepper halves, skin-side up, in a single layer on a baking sheet. Cook under the hot grill for 8–10 minutes, or until the skin is blackened and blistered all over. Using tongs, transfer to a polythene bag, tie the top and leave to cool. When cool enough to handle, peel off the skin.

2 Finely chop 1 of the garlic cloves. Place in a food processor or blender with the pepper halves, capers, parsley, lemon juice, cumin and sugar and process until smooth. Scrape into a bowl and stir in the olives.

3 Cut off and discard the crusty ends of the bread, then cut the bread into 1-cm/½-inch slices. Toast the slices on both sides. Cut the remaining garlic cloves in half, then rub the cut sides all over the toast. Brush the toast with the olive oil.

4 Spoon the red pepper mixture onto the toasted bread and place on a large serving platter. Serve immediately.

onion & olive rounds

serves four–eight

2 tbsp olive oil

1 onion, thinly sliced

1 garlic clove, finely chopped

2 tsp chopped fresh thyme

1 small French bread

1 tbsp tapenade or butter

8 canned anchovy fillets in oil, drained

12 olives stuffed with almonds or onion, halved

salt and pepper

COOK'S TIP

Tapenade is, strictly speaking, a French paste made from black olives and capers, but it adds immeasurably to the flavour of this tapa. Olives stuffed with almonds or onion are Spanish specialities, but if you can't find them, use pimiento- or anchovy-stuffed olives, or just stoned, black olives.

1 Heat the olive oil in a heavy-based frying pan. Add the onion and garlic and cook over a low heat, stirring occasionally, for 15 minutes, or until golden brown and very soft. Stir in the thyme and season to taste with salt and pepper.

2 Meanwhile, cut off and discard the crusty ends of the bread, then cut the loaf into 8 slices. Toast on both sides, then spread with tapenade or butter.

3 Pile the onion mixture on to the slices of toast and top each slice with an anchovy fillet and the olives. Serve hot.

prawn & haricot toasties

serves four

3 garlic cloves

4 tbsp olive oil

1 Spanish onion, halved and
finely chopped

400 g/14 oz canned haricot beans,
drained and rinsed

4 tomatoes, diced

4 thick slices country bread

280 g/10 oz cooked peeled prawns

salt and pepper

watercress, to garnish

1 Halve 1 of the garlic cloves and reserve. Finely chop the remaining cloves. Heat 2 tablespoons of the olive oil in a large, heavy-based frying pan. Add the chopped garlic and onion and cook over a low heat, stirring occasionally, for 5 minutes, or until softened.

2 Stir in the beans and tomatoes and season to taste with salt and pepper. Cook gently for a further 5 minutes.

3 Meanwhile, toast the bread on both sides, then rub each slice with the cut sides of the reserved garlic and drizzle with the remaining oil.

4 Stir the prawns into the bean mixture and heat through gently for 2–3 minutes. Pile the bean and prawn mixture onto the toasts and serve immediately, garnished with watercress.

aubergine & goat's cheese toasties

serves four

5 tbsp olive oil

2 aubergines, sliced

2 tomatoes, halved

2 tsp chopped fresh thyme

115 g/4 oz goat's cheese, crumbled

4 thick slices country bread

1 garlic clove, halved

salt and pepper

1 Heat a griddle pan and brush with 1 tablespoon of the olive oil. Add the aubergine slices and tomato halves and cook over a medium heat, turning occasionally, for 5 minutes. Transfer to a chopping board and roughly chop.

2 Transfer the aubergines to a bowl and stir in the thyme and about half the cheese. Drizzle with 2–3 tablespoons of the remaining olive oil and season to taste with salt and pepper, mixing well. Meanwhile, preheat the grill to medium.

3 Toast the bread under the hot grill on both sides, then rub each slice with the cut sides of the garlic and drizzle with the remaining oil.

4 Pile the aubergine mixture onto the toasts, spreading it out, and sprinkle with the remaining cheese. Cook under the hot grill for 2–3 minutes, or until hot and bubbling. Serve immediately.

COOK'S TIP

If you prefer, you can 'toast' the bread slices in the griddle pan rather than under the grill.

spanish spinach & tomato pizzas

makes thirty-two

2 tbsp Spanish olive oil, plus extra
    for brushing and drizzling

1 onion, finely chopped

1 garlic clove, finely chopped

400 g/14 oz canned chopped
    tomatoes

125 g/4½ oz fresh baby spinach

25 g/1 oz pine kernels

salt and pepper

BREAD DOUGH

100 ml/3½ fl oz warm water

½ tsp easy-blend dried yeast

pinch of sugar

200 g/7 oz strong white flour,
    plus extra for dusting

½ tsp salt

1 To make the bread dough, measure the water into a small bowl, sprinkle in the dried yeast and sugar and leave in a warm place for 10–15 minutes, or until frothy.

2 Meanwhile, sift the flour and salt into a large bowl. Make a well in the centre and pour in the yeast liquid, then mix together with a spoon. Using your hands, work the mixture until it leaves the sides of the bowl clean.

3 Turn the dough out onto a lightly floured work surface and knead for 10 minutes, or until smooth and elastic and no longer sticky. Shape into a ball and put it in a clean bowl. Cover with a clean, damp tea towel and leave in a warm place for 1 hour, or until it has risen and doubled in size.

4 To make the topping, heat the olive oil in a large, heavy-based frying pan. Add the onion and fry for 5 minutes, or until softened but not browned. Add the garlic and fry for a further 30 seconds. Stir in the tomatoes and cook for 5 minutes, letting it bubble and stirring occasionally, until reduced to a thick mixture. Add the spinach leaves and cook, stirring, until they have wilted slightly. Season to taste with salt and pepper.

5 While the dough is rising, preheat the oven to 200°C/400°F/ Gas Mark 6. Brush several baking sheets with olive oil. Turn the dough out onto a lightly floured work surface and knead well for 2–3 minutes to knock out the air bubbles.

6 Roll out the dough very, very thinly and, using a 6-cm/2½-inch plain, round cutter, cut out 32 rounds. Place on the prepared baking sheets.

7 Spread each base with the spinach mixture to cover, then sprinkle the pine kernels over the top. Drizzle a little olive oil over each pizza. Bake in the preheated oven for 10–15 minutes, or until the edges of the dough are golden brown. Serve the spinach and tomato pizzas hot.

chorizo pizza

serves four–six

6 tomatoes, sliced

2 onions, finely chopped

12 black olives

4 serrano ham slices

10 ready-to-eat chorizo
sausage slices

2 tbsp chopped mixed fresh herbs

55 g/2 oz Tronchon or mozzarella
cheese, thinly sliced

50 ml/2 fl oz olive oil

salt and pepper

PIZZA BASE

20 g/¾ oz fresh yeast

250 g/9 oz plain flour, plus extra
for dusting

225 ml/8 fl oz lukewarm water

pinch of salt

50 ml/2 fl oz olive oil

COOK'S TIP

Tronchon is a semi-soft cheese
from Aragon with a sharp and
aromatic flavour. It is very
popular for grilling and snacks in
Spain. If you can't find it, try
substituting Caerphilly for a
similar flavour and texture.

1 First make the pizza base. Mix the yeast with 55 g/2 oz of the flour and the water in a bowl. Leave to stand for 10 minutes.

2 Meanwhile, sift the remaining flour with the salt into a large bowl and make a well in the centre. Add the yeast mixture and the olive oil. Using an electric mixer, mix well for 5–10 minutes. Cover with a clean tea towel and leave in a warm place until the dough has doubled in size.

3 Preheat the oven to 220°C/ 425°F/Gas Mark 7 and place a baking sheet in the oven to warm. Pat out the pizza dough into a 28–30-cm/11–12-inch round on a lightly floured work surface and make a slightly raised rim around the edge.

4 Arrange the tomato slices on top of the pizza dough, season to taste with salt, then cover with the onion. Add the olives, ham and chorizo, then season to taste with pepper and sprinkle over the herbs. Top with the cheese slices and drizzle with the olive oil.

5 Carefully transfer the pizza to the preheated baking sheet and bake in the preheated oven for 30 minutes, or until the cheese has melted and is bubbling and the rim has lightly browned. Cut into wedges and serve.